PENNINE PEOPLE

Upper Slaithwaite Brass Band and Reed Band formed in 1892

Day out for the Scammonden councillors

PENNINE PEOPLE

*Clogs, Flat Caps and
Drip-bread for Breakfast*

H AZEL W HEELER

ALAN SUTTON PUBLISHING LIMITED

First published in the United Kingdom in 1994
Alan Sutton Publishing Ltd · Phoenix Mill · Far Thrupp · Stroud
Gloucestershire

First published in the United States of America in 1994
Alan Sutton Publishing Inc. · 83 Washington Street · Dover
NH 03820

British Library Cataloguing in Publication Data

A catalogue record for this book is available from the British
Library.

ISBN 0-7509-0713-4

Library of Congress Cataloging in Publication Data applied for.

Typeset in 12/13 Bembo.
Typesetting and origination by
Alan Sutton Publishing Limited.
Printed in Great Britain by
Ebenezer Baylis, Worcester.

CONTENTS

From left to right: Mary Sykes, aged 89, from Naze; Elizabeth France, aged 85, from Shawfield; Sarah Sykes, aged 82, from Spa Terrace; Maria Shaw, aged 80, from Bank Nook

CHAPTER ONE

CLARICE HAIGH REMEMBERS

The Pennine Chain, as we learn in the schoolroom, is the 'backbone of England'.

Pennine people, born and reared in bleak, isolated, moorland terrain, nevertheless had – and still have – the 'backbone' of character to match their surroundings. Despite hardship and early deaths, those who survived show an indomitable spirit, laced with a dry wit and ready humour. When you're not born with a silver spoon in your mouth, you have to draw on inner resources to make life tolerable. Simple pleasures, the minutiae of life, with all the fascination of even the most everyday things, are observed more keenly, and truly valued.

One such instance was Clarice Haigh's recollection of seeing a relative in his coffin. In life he had had a crooked nose; in death, it had straightened out. As in Handel's *Messiah*, so beloved in Pennine districts, maybe everywhere as time goes on, 'and the rough places plain' will become a reality.

Clarice was born on a smallholding at Lingards, Slaithwaite, in 1903. David, her father, was a weaver and excellent stone waller. Like most of his neighbours, he worked hard and had only two days holiday for Easter, Whitsuntide, and Christmas. One Yuletide he had 12 shillings to pay for everything. Armed with the frugal sum, down into Slaithwaite went Mrs Haigh, desperate to buy a few festive gifts for her six children. She returned with six little spice pigs with curly string tails, an orange, nuts, and a shiny new penny for each of her offspring, then she wrapped up six pieces of Christmas cake to bulk out the six black woollen stockings that hung expectantly over the bed rails.

Clarice's grandad, William Ainley, wove in his own home at Scapegoat Hill; he was especially fond of one of her brothers,

Clough Head Baptist Sunday School pupils. From left to right: Ruby, Clarice and Ethel Haigh

John. 'Grandad's little pal' he affectionately called the child. Unfortunately, in 1908 John fell ill with croup. Although a croup kettle was kept steaming continuously in the cottage, it proved a vain attempt to revive the ailing child – a youngster who resembled Millais' Bubbles with fair curls.

'Tha'll get better lad,' Grandad Ainley kept reassuring his grandson. But it wasn't to be. That Good Friday his little pal passed away.

Clarice was barely two when she used to toddle across to Lingards School, where Miss Eagland was a teacher. Amelia, her eldest sister, was a pupil there, and Clarice wanted to be with her.

Every autumn the family killed a pig, and one year they managed to fatten the animal to an astonishing sixteen stone. Once slaughtered, coarse salt was pushed inside the ham for two or three weeks before it was hung up. Dried and blown up pigs' bladders sealed with string made excellent hard footballs. Nothing that could be used was ever wasted.

Liver and bacon in jam jars made acceptable gifts for relations, shop bought gifts being beyond their means. Yet, despite their poverty, they were happy, and occasionally there were treats. When brother Harold started courting, he bought a box of chocolates for the girls, and rewarded Clarice with a penny for cleaning his shoes.

In wintertime, when the children wore clogs for school – excellent for sliding – concerts were held at Clough Head School and there was carol singing with the Clough Head chapel, also carols on New Year's Eve. The singers would meet at chapel at 9.00 p.m., a custom that persisted right up to the Second World War. One of the New Year's Eve carols they sang as they walked the hilly district went 'Behold, Behold, another rolling year, Has swiftly passed away', which was repeated three times, followed by 'And we within Thy Courts Appear, To Hail this Happy Day', also repeated. Another favourite old carol was 'Listen to the Wondrous Story Which we chant in Hymns of Joy'.

At some point during the First World War Amelia read in a magazine how to make a big Christmas cracker with a little present for everyone hidden inside, the whole attached to ribbons of different colours. The cracker was duly made from green crêpe paper, a majestic sight suspended horizontally from

A concert at Clough Head in the 1920s

Starlight concert party. Clarice is seated in the front row, second from left

the ceiling. That Christmas Clarice thought her gift of red leather slippers absolutely wonderful.

When she left school, along with most of her friends Clarice worked in Joseph Hoyle's mill. Then came the slump of 1926. Arthur Moore of Dundas Street, Huddersfield, advertised for workers to go out to a mill in Perth, Ontario. People were desperate for work. Mr Moore loaned money for the outward journey to those prepared to go. Clarice was one of the intrepid ones who took up his offer and set forth on the great adventure. The millworkers sailed out on the *Regina*. Once they arrived in Canada they still had to travel another 200 miles by train to Perth where they stayed in an hotel until they found accommodation. What a revelation the Canadian scenery must have been for those Pennine folk after a lifetime of seeing nothing but the landscape of northern England! 'Even the robins are bigger than ours,' noted the awestruck Clarice.

The mending room of Tayside Textiles overlooked a picturesque lawn and river, and the operatives could see boats sailing up and down as they worked. It had been a rough voyage. Harvey Rothery, a tuner, was sick for a whole week

Clarice (seated right) in Canada, 1926

that October in 1926. Perhaps that was why he, and a few others, decided to forsake their Pennine homeland and stay in Canada all their lives rather than repeat their terrible journey.

But Clarice Haigh eventually returned to live in Bolster Moor. She had made many friends while working in Canada, and happily went back for holidays when she could. The pull of the Pennines, however, proved too strong for her to contemplate living anywhere else for too long.

CHAPTER TWO

LIFE FOR THE SHAWS OF WATROYD FARM

Haigh is a name often heard in the Colne Valley area of the Pennines. Lilian Shaw, Haigh when she married, was born at Watroyd Farm, Golcar, on 25 May 1902. Her father, John Alfred, started out as a teamer earning a guinea a week. He grew corn, scattering seed from a basket over the fields. Often he would quote from the Bible: 'He who soweth shall also reap,' adding humorously, – 'and if I don't reap I shall never believe the Bible again.' He had occasion to believe in miracles, though. In 1910, during a heavy snowfall, the mistal roof fell in. Yet not one of his cattle was hurt, and a kindly neighbouring farmer allowed him to house them temporarily on his premises.

John Alfred had seven children, of whom two had died. Lilian was the youngest of the surviving ones. One Christmas she longed for a blackboard, and pencilled a letter to Santa Claus with her request. Alas, a few days before the red-cloaked old gentleman was due Lilian found a blackboard beneath her bed, 'And the bottom of my world fell out,' she said. But there were other high points. Lilian's parents always managed to save £20 so that their children could have new clothes for Whitsuntide.

A lifetime of hard work and thrift did not seem to harm Mr Shaw – he never once needed to see the doctor. If he had two extra horses to attend to he earned two more shillings. Often he drove a horse and cart to Manchester in the early hours, his way lit by the cart's oil lamps, passing through the Standedge cutting on his way to get corn, seeing tramps sleeping by the roadside. One advantage of the rough, unmade roads of those days was that horses didn't slip as much on icy wintry mornings.

Occasionally, John Alfred halted at the Olive Branch pub on the return journey. Landlord John Sykes did not condone customers spending money on drink if they had children, so they were asked, 'Has ta any childer?' If they said yes, Sykes ordered, 'Tak' thi brass home, Ah don't serve beer to men who have families to provide for.' But they were welcome to drink water if they wished.

When Lilian was ten she badly wanted a swimming costume, but her mother couldn't afford to buy one. Undaunted, the child cut the feet off some old black Botany wool stockings, opened them up, and stitched them together into the semblance of a costume. Mrs Haigh was so upset at seeing her daughter's desperate efforts that she went to the unusual expense of buying a costume, and Lilian sported it proudly in Slaithwaite Baths.

John Alfred also had a milk round in Golcar, and milk, still warm from the cow, was the staple drink at their home. He also kept pigs and hens. A passer-by who asked for John Alfred was directed, 'Father's in the pig sty, you'll know him by his hat.'

Lilian attended Clough Head Baptist Sunday School twice on Sundays, then went to the evening service at church. In those days everybody went to Sunday school and there were twenty-four Sunday school teachers in Golcar.

The Shaw family. Left to right: Willie, Lilian, John Alfred, Elizabeth Mary, Gertrude

Clough Head Christmas Day concert featuring the 'action song' 'Milkmaids'

Clough Head always put on a Christmas Day concert and the children practised for weeks beforehand. It began at seven in the evening, performers and audience walking there and back in pitch blackness, unless there was a moon. They featured a number of 'action songs', one entitled, appropriately enough, 'Milkmaids'.

One year Lilian's young brother, Dyson Shaw, demanded to take part in the entertainment. He was all togged up in best knickerbocker suit and wing collar. No one could restrain his enthusiasm so the minister encouraged him to 'do his turn' as he took the centre of the stage.

'I have a little spade—' faltered the youthful entertainer.

'Go on, my little man,' urged the minister. But that was all the shamefaced little boy could manage.

They never had turkey at Christmas, only roast beef. Elizabeth Mary, Mrs Shaw, baked every Tuesday, carrying teacakes balanced along the length of her arm into the stone breadpot in the cellar. Only when visitors called did they have 'proper' cake, 'everyday teas' ending instead with a kind of currant teacake made from sweetened dough.

Mrs Shaw's father lived with them. Grandad loved to sit in his corner by the Dutch oven. There was a hook down the chimney which he used for cooking bacon over the heat from the coals, dropping cheese into the dripping for his breakfast.

Lighting was from oil lamps for there was no electricity on the farm until the 1920s. On Sunday mornings Lilian's father milked twenty-eight cows before donning his best suit for the walk to Pole Moor chapel. Elizabeth, her mother, remained at the farm to cook a piece of inlift, although she never ate any herself at mid-day. She didn't want to risk having a 'heavy stomach' as she faced the long walk to chapel in the afternoon so she waited and had bread and cold meat when she got home.

Invariably, breakfast for the children was oatmeal porridge, with lashings of milk. In the kitchen was a big bath where milk churns were placed to cool.

Up at the school, the children used slates to write on, pinning a bit of rag to their dresses or jerseys to clean them with. Sometimes a teacher asked Lilian to wash up. There was only cold water, but a child could earn a halfpenny a week for the work. Although there were no school dinners, so no plates or cutlery, the tin mugs still had to be rinsed out.

In wet and wintry weather pupils' clogs were inspected every

Clough Head Council School, Golcar, June 1918. Clarice Haigh is seated fourth right, front row, while Lilian Shaw is standing third from right in the third row (with two ribbons in her hair)

morning to see if they were clean. How Lilian envied one girl – her clogs had copper ends at the toes. If Lilian's clogs needed new irons, she was secretly delighted – it meant she could attend weekday school in her Sunday best lace-up boots. Nor were there sandals for summertime in those days. As for the rest of their clothing, her mother knitted bonnets for her children, and made most of their clothes, apart from the Whitsuntide ones and straw hats.

Near the school was a little shop, Weavills. One of Lilian's school friends used to say fervently during the Lord's Prayer: 'And deliver us from Weavills.'

Children adored Whit Monday, walking behind the brass band. Here is one of the ditties they chanted as they played games in a field after their Whit Monday outings:

Oats and beans and barley (*repeat*)
Open the ring, and choose one in,
    And kiss her when you've got her in
And now you're married you must obey
You must be kind in all you say
    And help your wife to chop the wood. (*repeated three times*)

When Lilian passed the County Minor Examination, she went on to Greenhead Municipal High School for Girls, entailing a walk to Golcar Station every morning. How delicious she found the tomato and potato pies on the menu at Greenhead for school dinners compared to her usual fare!

Reminiscent of her childhood wish for a blackboard was her ambition to become a school teacher. In those days, when school teachers were looked up to with something akin to deference and awe, teaching was still considered a desirable profession and one which conferred a definite status.

After completing her training at Bingley College, where the young ladies were required 'to put their hair up' since no schoolmistress could be expected to inspire discipline among her young pupils if her hair was flowing down her back, Lilian's teaching career commenced at Lingards. To reach Lingards she had to cross a quarry through which the Watroyd Farm dog Shep daily escorted her safely as far as the main road. Afterwards he dutifully returned to the farm. If she was

Students at Bingley College. Lilian is
seated in the middle

late, the tram driver would obligingly cross the road to look
for the young teacher.

In 1923 the result of her final examinations was due. Neither
the farm nor Lingards School, where she was a trainee teacher,
possessed a telephone. So, unable to wait until tea time to hear if
she had passed, Lilian devised an ingenious way of finding out.
She asked her father to pin a sheet of newspaper to the gable end
of the farm if she had been successful so she would see it when
she went outside at playtime. When the letter arrived with the
good news, her father was so proud he nailed the biggest white
tablecloth he could find to that gable end! When the young
teacher looked anxiously across the valley, there was the white
emblem silently transmitting the marvellous news. It was one of
the highlights of Miss Shaw's life. And when Mallinson's Mill
buzzer shrilled at five, even Shep, bounding across the quarry to
meet her, seemed to have an extra wag to his tail as he greeted
his young mistress.

Each generation of schoolchildren played the same games. At
Clough Head was a big smooth slab of stone where Lilian and
her friends played 'jacks', a game which the local children called
'jecks'. The blacksmith fashioned iron bullies for the lads to roll,
girls had wooden ones. Lilian kept hers throughout her long life.

Her mother helped finances by making butter, dipping her
hand into nearly boiling water to prevent the butter from
sticking to it. The imprint of a cow adorned the finished pats.

Grandad Shaw was an integral, well-loved member of the family and Lilian enjoyed playing draughts, dominoes and ludo with him in her leisure time. When electric lighting became generally available, her brother Dyson canvassed the district, persuading householders to agree to have the 'new-fangled' illumination installed.

Lilian and her family used to sit round the fire on winter evenings, playing board games, talking and listening to advice, not least among which was the injunction never to buy what they could not afford on the easy payment system. 'Buy now, pay later,' was regarded as an entirely wrong way of life.

Going up to bed after one such pleasant evening, Lilian recalls a funny little incident. In the thirties eiderdowns and lace bedspreads were popular. And not only with people. Lilian had a tremendous shock when she discovered a fieldmouse, its head entangled in the intricate pattern of her own lace bedspread. One of the penalties of living in the country.

At Watroyd Farm cows were always turned into the fields on 14 May and it was on that date, in 1932, that Lilian had her

Lilian and Joe at Watroyd Farm, 1932

Lilian and Joe on their wedding day

wedding day. That glorious Whitsuntide the reception was held at Watroyd Farm. Lilian was thirty, husband Joe, a butcher, thirty-two. As female teachers had to resign on marriage, Lilian would now have to take on all the household duties. The new bride had no experience of washing, as her mother had sent hers to a washerwoman. But the newly weds had bought an electric Beatty washer, and only knew of three other such wonderful household aids owned in the whole locality. Lilian's aunt looked at it with reverence. 'Ee, Luv, if I had one of those I'd take in washing.' Including discount, it had cost £32 16s. from the Hill Top Co-op. A Jacobean bookcase was bought for £9 15s., a mirror (still in Mrs Haigh's home) for £2 13s. 6d., and a piano for £78 15s. What delightful hours were spent playing on that! 'The Robin's Return', 'The William Tell Overture', Weber's 'Invitation to the Waltz' – music that gave endless pleasure. When the couple's son John was young, Lilian entertained him in the afternoons playing those lilting melodies.

On that May afternoon in 1932 she presented her groom with two volumes of Burns's letters. Joe loved verse, and when the couple were out walking on the moors often 'burst out into poetry'. One of their well loved books was *The Oxford Book of Carols*, first published in 1928. Lilian loved the Mothering Sunday carol 'He Who Goes a Mothering Finds Violets in the Lane':

It is the day of all the year, Of all the year the one day
When I shall see my Mother dear, And bring her cheer,
A mothering on Sunday. So I'll put on my Sunday coat,
And in my hat a feather, And get the lines I write by rote
With many a note, That I've strung together.
And now to fetch my wheaten cake,
To fetch it from the baker,
He promised me, for Mother's sake, The best he'd bake,
For me to fetch and take her.
Well have I known, as I went by, One hollow lane,
that none day
I'd fail to find – for all they're shy – Where violets lie,
As I went home on Sunday.
My sister Jane is waiting-maid, Along with Squire's lady,
And year by year her part she's played, And home she stayed,
To get the dinner ready.
For Mother'll come to church, you'll see –
Of all the year it is the day
The one she'll say, that's made for me. And so it be,
It's every Mother's free day
The boys will all come home from town, Not one will miss that
one day
And every maid will bustle down, To show her gown,
A-Mothering on Sunday.
It is the day of all the year, Of all the year one day.
And here come I, my Mother dear, To bring you cheer,
A-Mothering on Sunday.

CHAPTER THREE

SOCIAL LIFE AT SHRED

Born on Christmas Day 1911 near Nont Sarah's, up on the moors, Horace Hirst has been a cycling fan from boyhood. Living in a listed seventeenth-century cottage below Moorside Edge radio station now, with his wife Annie, the sprightly octogenarian still bikes down to Slaithwaite for his newspaper – his home is far too distant and isolated for it to be worthwhile a newsagent delivering. 'It's a fair way to push it back, but it's nice going down,' laughs Horace. When not in use, the bike is 'kept in't coal hole'.

Horace's dad died when he was three, his younger sister when she was five. He still remembers wondering why everything had gone quiet, then seeing the little girl with a white handkerchief over her face. She is buried in Pole Moor cemetery. The widowed Mrs Hirst went out cleaning and also took in washing. They kept a few hens for their eggs and as a treat would eat one of the hens for Christmas dinner. To make ends meet, Horace's mother also baked for people, including the Nont Sarah's public house. Two servants carrying wicker clothes baskets used to collect her confectionery, which had been baked on the black Yorkshire range.

Percy Jakeman and Horace Hirst (left) at Slaithwaite Carnival in the 1970s

Horace attended Wilberlee Council School, half an hour's walk away from his home. When deep snowdrifts levelled the landscape, he could walk to school in a direct line, on top of the dry stone walls. But he welcomed the days when it was impossible to negotiate the drifts as the headmaster, Mr Falkener, struck terror into his pupils. He was fonder of spiders. Indeed, such a connoisseur of these insects was he that 'The Spiderman'

Horace Hirst at Pleasant
Pastures in the 1930s

had one named after him – Falkener Hero. One
morning a school child came across his headmaster
lying full-length over a brook. He thought he must
have collapsed, but on closer inspection it proved
that Mr Falkener was simply intent on observing a
spider.

Horace recalls how on chilly winter days when
he and the others went to school they took hot
cinders in a tin can to warm their hands on. They
would also take something to eat for mid-day,
putting their plates on the classroom pipes to warm
the food up a bit. Of course, Falkener's stick 'used
to be plyed regular away' – something guaranteed
to warm hands up more than anything.

Horace never went away for a holiday until he left school.
Then he and two other youths decided to cycle to Blackpool.
When one turned up at the start of the journey Horace asked,
'Where's thi portmanteau?' After all, they were intending to stay
for a day or two. 'I have it in me pocket,' came the reply. Usually
they just went to Sunny Vale or Hope Bank for the day, so
preparations for a real holiday were something of which most
people had hardly any experience.

Working days were spent spinning at Pogson's Mill in
Slaithwaite, his leisure hours being passed as a non-playing
member in Slaithwaite Brass Band Room.

Two local girls celebrated birthdays on Christmas Day as well
as Horace. All three VIPs would walk down to the Christmas
tree in Slaithwaite. Invariably, someone turned up and started
conducting carols, at midnight striking up a rousing 'Christians
Awake'. Every year there was the same ritual, followed by the
long walk home over hilly paths after everyone had sung 'Happy
Birthday to You'. The rest of the year, amusements at home
were games of tiddleywinks, cards, ludo, draughts and beggar-
my-neighbour. More sophisticated toys were considered
expensive luxuries so when one Christmas as a lad Horace
received a Meccano set, it was appreciated as a truly memorable
gift.

'Shred' chapel, so called after the land it was built on, was the
focal point of the area, and Horace a life-long member. At

'Shred' chapel, Slaithwaite

Whitsuntide the tradition was that districts took it in turn to march first behind the brass band: Upper Slaithwaite at the front one year, West another time. Social life revolved round Shred: the Easter sale of work was held there regularly and there are fond memories of preparing stalls and teas for it during the 1930s, of 'dressing up' after the mid-day dinner then going back again. Old scholars or similar local celebrities were invited to open the event, and everyone always hoped for fine weather. They laid great store by country folklore and such sayings as 'If it rains on Palm Sunday, it's fine on Easter Sunday.'

Horace's chum, Harold Haigh, had a sister, Annie. Horace and Annie began courting, going for walks and attending plays and concerts together at Shred. Annie, who later became his wife, is the great granddaughter of the Pennine 'Quack Doctor' Dick of Merrydale, whose sister Nancy went as a servant to Doctor William Dean. Nancy was a comely twenty, Doctor Dean's son a fresh-faced nineteen. She became pregnant, and they married and went to live in a back cottage at Merrydale. They produced four sons, all of whom became doctors.

Originally Dick had been a farmer, but he became interested in herbalism and attended classes eventually putting 'MD' after his name, stating cockily that it merely stood for Merrydale Dick and 'They know nowt i' London.' Many a tale is told of Dick's 'professional' activities. One day a patient approached the self-styled doctor, gingerly holding out her injured finger for inspection. As Dick leaned forward to see the afflicted member, it was quickly pulled away. 'Put thi shawl on Mary Jane, and go 'whom,' she was commanded. Another story tells how a relative of Annie's, when three years old, scalded his hand in boiling jam as his mother was stirring it in a big pan. She dropped everything, hurrying the little lad to see Dick of Merrydale. After examining the child, Dick got up and went into a field, returning with some warm cow dung. Tenderly he plastered it over each tiny finger before bandaging them. 'Don't remove them for six weeks,' were his instructions. When the child returned and the bandages were removed, there wasn't a burn mark to be seen.

One of the books Merrydale Dick referred to was *Culpepper's Complete Herbal*, not exactly orthodox medical reading. The Marsden poet Samuel Laycock wrote this tribute to his friend, who died in his seventy-ninth year, in 1886, and is buried in Slaithwaite churchyard.

> In Memory of Richard Horsfall
> Lay this tribute of love on the breast of my friend
>   That the song of the land with his ashes may blend,
> Oh Merrydale! Long hadst thou cause to be glad
> But a friend has been ta'en and tis well thou art sad.
>   The flowers bloom on in the dell as of yore,
> But the worthy old doctor will see them no more.
>   Fare well! Till we see thee again in that glade
> Where the song never ends and the flowers never fade.

The cause of the good doctor's death occurred when a brook burst its banks. To stop the flooding Dick went to attend to the matter, no Wellingtons or even clogs on his feet. Careless of his own well-being, he became soaked through, and succumbed to pneumonia.

Great granddaughter Annie was brought up in the cottage next to where she lives today. She has known Horace, her husband, since they were babies. They attended the same Wilberlee School, and were equally terrified of 'The 'owd Arrin' (the old spider) as headmaster Falkener was known. When it was time for the County Minor Scholarship examination, Annie's name was put forward. But Falkener told her, 'It's no good you going in for it, you won't pass.' But this seeming setback mattered little then – getting work was the main objective of most school leavers in those days.

So Annie became a weaver, making the acquaintance of the mill engine affectionately called Elizabeth, toiling from seven till five, with half an hour, from 8.30 to 9.00 a.m. allowed for breakfast which was eaten at the side of her loom. At dinnertime she went down into the 'fire hole' where the boiler was and where she had put the enamel dish of food she had brought to warm up. If she forgot to put the dish on some time before dinner, it wouldn't be ready and would have to be consumed cold and unappetizing.

Horace's sister also worked in the mill. One day she took bread sauce for her dinner, something Annie had never encountered before; she wondered what it was. Mill buzzers sounded at 6.30 a.m., and if an employee was late he or she was locked out till breakfast time. Then, shamed, they had to go through the office and 'be recognized' by those who worked at Globe Mill.

Drifting snow was no deterrent to Annie and her ilk – they simply jumped into it, negotiating their way to work as best they could in the winter gloom. Annie was the first to own black wellingtons up there, which must have at least kept her feet dry in the often grim weather. Indeed, some winter mornings the loom handles were so perishingly cold they felt to be burning her hands. The girls wore black overalls at work, earning 30 shillings in the late 1920s for a gruelling week's work. Then Harold Macmillan docked 10 per cent off all textile workers wages.

Perhaps because of their shared hardships, people were honest. Overalls were left on nails in the wall, and Annie remembers keeping a pair of scissors in hers; nothing was locked away. If her scissors were borrowed, they were always put back. Her mother, Sarah Alice France, still made all her clothes.

In June 1908 Sarah's sister, Elizabeth France, passed away aged ninety-one, never having had more than two bottles of medicine in her life. On her ninetieth birthday her eyesight had still been good enough for her to make a pin cushion for each of her twenty grandchildren without the aid of spectacles. She too was interred at Slaithwaite.

At Cockley Cote, Moorside Edge, Annie's grandparents brought up twelve children. Upstairs was the loom and at bedtime an old door was placed across it, and mattresses filled with hay served for some to sleep on. The parents slept in a bed that turned up against the wall during daylight hours, in the downstairs rooms. To this day one can still see part of the loom in the attic.

The eldest son went to America, earning a living cutting down trees in Kalamazoo. In their veritable treasure trove of an attic is retained Annie's grandfather's frock coat which neighbour Ruth Denby, aged ninety-two, wore at local chapel Shred's garden party in 1992, set off by a top hat made from cardboard and black paint. Annie's great grandmother's cape also reposes in the attic along with other mementoes. In the cottage a German clock, another keepsake, plays 'Highland Mary' on the hour.

Annie had a strict upbringing – she wasn't even allowed to go

Elizabeth France

to Slaithwaite Band Room unless her brother went with her. Nevertheless, there were opportunities for fun. Shred chapel organized a whist drive and dance and social evenings on a Saturday. Then there was the 'Monkey Run' up the Nonts road, where young lasses and lads strolled to meet each other, dressed in their Sunday best. Those were Annie's only leisure outlets, and before she left she was always cautioned, 'You'll come back with Harold won't you?' 'But,' Annie twinkles, 'my brother had mates—'.

Horace's mother, Ida, used to walk all the way from Moorlands to Cunning Corner at Rishworth to work in a cotton mill when she was a young girl, trudging along hills like a switchback, with rough, unmade paths, wearing long petticoats and clogs. Yet hard work in mills and long moorland trudges did nothing to deflect from the communities' enthusiasm for the Slaithwaite Band. It brought fame to that village by winning championship trophies, including high honours at Crystal Palace in 1905 and 1933 and Manchester Belle Vue in 1938.

Initially a working man's band, its members would gather to spend a strenuous couple of hours rehearsing after a full day in the loom gate or workshop when an important contest was in the offing. The band was formed in 1892 at Shred School, on

Ida Hirst

the hillside a mile or so above Slaithwaite and rejoiced in the name Upper Slaithwaite Brass and Reed Band. It enjoyed its heyday at a time when there was neither wireless nor cinema and Pennine people organized their own entertainment.

It had been the activities of a Black and White Minstrel Group attached to the school which originally put the idea of forming a brass and reed band into the minds of the first members. Concerts, dances and other entertainments were held to raise funds and despite severe weather and the anxiety caused by slackness of work, all were well patronized. Such willing support was especially commendable when one recalls that there was no public transport to Wilberlee then.

A programme for a concert held in Shred School on 29 October 1892 sounds well worth the effort of getting there. It opened with a march played by the band, 'See the Clouds are Gently Breaking', which was followed by a song by Mr J. Hirst, 'England, the Land of the Free'. Then came something a bit more risqué – 'The Kiss behind the Door' sung by Mr Tom Sykes. Later, a dialogue with six characters, 'Coaxed and Hoaxed', was performed. Messrs Delbert Haigh and Chas. Wm. Haigh played a cornet duet, 'Honest and True', then a duet was sung by Miss S.A. Hirst and Mr H. Haigh entitled 'Folly and Fashion'. The band gave a selection, 'The Minstrel', followed by a reading 'Yar Emma' by Mr W.H. Haigh. Afterwards came 'Shaving Done Here', a dialogue for five characters. The whole, ambitious event ended with a splendid glee by the band, entitled 'Hours of Beauty' rising to a stirring conclusion with 'God Save the Queen'. Nor were the closing moments disturbed by a single member of the audience dashing out to catch their bus, for there weren't any. And, certainly, nobody owned a car. So all stood solemnly to attention to applaud the virtuoso performance. At the piano were Messrs J. Bamforth and J.W. France, and the conductor was Mr Delbert Haigh. One penny a week had been contributed towards the funds by bandsmen, their wives, sweethearts and friends.

The first parade of the band was from Shred School to the Rose and Crown, Cophill, Slaithwaite – it must have been quite some march if one considers the condition of those moorland roads. Often the route was blocked by boulders, scattered here and there, elsewhere the surface had been washed away, and there were, too, the deep ruts made by cartwheels to negotiate. However, obstacles overcome made for a greater sense of achievement, and more gusto infused into the triumphant marches played by that indomitable group of men.

Any such group is bound to have its practical joker. Once a bandsman brought a couple of guinea pigs to rehearsal. During the interval someone put the rodents down the bell of the brass band flat bass. When practice resumed, the music was duly augmented by anguished squeals from the guinea pigs. The guilty player was threatened with suspension by the conductor, but he too was soon overcome with laughter. One can only hope that the poor little victims managed to appreciate the funny side of it as well. . . .

The Pennine character is such that setbacks only seem to promote an even greater determination to succeed. They refuse to be discouraged by the sorts of difficulty that would tend to make others give up trying. For instance, it was far from a pleasure trip going to the Crystal Palace in 1933. Finances had first to be managed, which was solved by holding a carnival promoted by the band. Then followed five weeks of rehearsals, right up to the Friday night prior to the contest. And all the band members put in their usual day's work before a two hour rehearsal. Lady helpers served a hot stew to the bandsmen before they set off on their night-long journey to London, where they arrived at about 6.00 a.m. It wouldn't have been a comfortable ride. There followed a light breakfast, a brief rehearsal to 'blow the cobwebs away', a fleeting look round a few of the sights then off to Sydenham, only to learn that their band had been drawn last to play out of twenty competitors.

At the close of the long day of that great massed bands concert some forty thousand listeners cheered to the rafters. Then came the announcement of the winners. Slaithwaite Band had emerged victorious by a margin of ten points. How proud they were, how worthwhile everyone's efforts had proved!

In recognition of their particular contributions to the band's success, on 21 January 1933 presentations were made to Mr Ben Sykes, bass trombone player, who had joined the band when it was formed in 1892. He received the bass trombone on which he had played for over twenty years, besides a trouser press and smoking cabinet. Mr Herbert Eastwood received an inscribed gold medal and walking stick for stalwart work in support of the band during the preceding five years.

Sales of work were frequently held to defray the cost of new uniforms. On winning the championship contest at Belle Vue on 4 September 1938, Slaithwaite was awarded the £2,000 gold trophy, the *Sunday Chronicle* championship prize, £100 cash, a gold medal, a special prize of a brass instrument valued at 15 guineas, a further special prize of a brown leather attaché case, value 3 guineas, plus two additional special medal prizes.

This time the contest began at 1.00 p.m. and Slaithwaite had again been drawn to play towards the close, last but one of twenty-three. It was almost seven o'clock when, at long last, they mounted the platform. The test piece was 'Owain Glyndwr'. When the results were announced, Slaithwaite was again first, followed by Black Dyke in second place, Luton in third, in fourth Besses O' the' Barn, in fifth Edge Hill LMS, sixth the famous Brighouse and Rastrick.

When a telephone message with news of the band's triumph was received in Slaithwaite, the village went wild with excitement. On their return, still 'fit as fiddles' the band left their motor coach at Ned Lane at 10.15 p.m., and paraded along Britannia Road, Carr Lane, Crimble Bank, and along Hill Top to their band room playing inspiring marches along the route to the accompaniment of tremendous cheering. And for the band there was another highlight in the offing – their first prize success brought with it a broadcasting engagement at Leeds two days after the concert.

When the band moved to new premises at Clough House from Shred, the committee bought the instruments and equipment of the old Slaithwaite Band. They played for Slaithwaite Parish Church in every Whit Monday procession from 1898 to 1937 (no procession was held by the church on that Whit Monday of 1937). For years, starting on New Year's Eve 1933, the band took part in a special musical service held on the last Sunday evening of the old year in Slaithwaite Parish Church. These occasions were some of the highlights of the musical year in the Colne Valley. The band also gave their services at many functions held to obtain funds for charities, and Comforts Funds during both world wars. They were noted, too, for their annual outdoor 'Sing' at Merrydale.

CHAPTER FOUR

TALES FROM THE PUB

A different type of Pennine clientele prefers pubs to chapels. Moorland inns are ideal spots to 'down a pint' and listen to tales of some of the characters who enlivened the vast, bleak open spaces with their odd quirks of behaviour.

Up at the White House, on the moors above Slaithwaite, brothers William and Archie lived in a house named Top O' Th' Hill. In the 1930s the lads had a squabble about a hen. They fell out, and though continuing to live in the same house, never addressed another word to each other.

Their day-to-day requirements, such as shopping, were attended to by housekeeper Annie Sykes. She bought the food, demanding half each of the 'brass' needed. The brothers ate their meals separately, in stony silence. Yet when Archie was informed by some joker that William had dropped down dead at the mill, he was full of brotherly concern, even having the flag on the British Legion premises hauled down to half-mast. Discovering that William was still alive at home, Archie was furious at being made a fool of. Nevertheless, he 'said nowt', and resumed the long silence. William, after quaffing his fill at the White House, frequently baulked at the prospect of dragging his weary legs up the steep hill home. Instead, he would drape himself in a prominent position on the roadside, where, feigning illness – 'Ee, ah am badly' – he was usually picked up by the sympathetic driver of a passing horse and cart and driven home.

The brothers had their own seats at the pub, and woe betide any interloper who dared sit on one. Archie, who died in 1968, used to tap any such intruder with his stick. Actions spoke louder than words.

To that same pub Luke Howley used to take his border collie,

Derek Walker (in the flat cap) and his pals outside the White House in the 1980s

Lassie. There the dog sat happily beneath one of the tables, patiently waiting until his master decided to go home. Another regular, John William Shaw Walker, and Luke gave the impression of being sworn enemies, such was the verbal abuse that passed between them, but in reality they were the best of pals. One day Luke set out with his horse and float to deliver milk at Marsden. Unfortunately for his master, the horse failed to negotiate a tricky bend on thin ice. It bolted, hurtling Luke unceremoniously over the black dry stone wall. Another milkman happened to be passing the scene of the mishap on his round and bawled out, 'Ah thowt tha were practising for Beecher's, lad.'

Those were the days of sawdust on pub floors, and spittoons. In the 1930s a local, Chuck Storey, bundled a foal into the pub to christen it. Chuck, dressed in landlady Dorothy Blakeley's nightie (to pretend he was a parson), poured whisky over the astounded foal's head, christening it Wilkie Bard; the startled animal was one of three foals to be similarly christened in that decade. When the landlady, who had presided over many such stunts died, a service in her memory was held at the White House, and her ashes were scattered in the vicinity.

A fancy dress event was staged at the pub in the 1950s. At one memorable point Jack O' Sacky's dressed up as a lady and went out to the two-seater lavatory, 'a double header'. What a shock the other lady had when, by the light of Jack's candle, stuck in a jam jar, she realized that her companion was a man!

On the rugged moorland a shepherd and his dog were once a common sight. One such duo was George Mitchell and his sheep dog, Glen. They were like something straight out of a scene from *One Man and His Dog*. The pair enjoyed many successes, including winning the Kilnsey Show in the 1980s. When drinkers gather to relate a few yarns, one of the tales buzzing around is the old chestnut that flatulence from a single sheep can create enough methane gas to power a small lorry for 25 miles – sheep, apparently, are parted from their 'goods' quicker than a Yorkshireman is parted from his brass!

Many years ago two farmers, brothers who lived in Meltham, decided to brew their own beer and their farmhouse was eventually transformed into The Traveller's Rest public house. An old publican always kept a stewpan on the fire in the tap room. It smelt delicious, except, that is, for those who knew its history – it was kept topped up with anything and everything. Dead hens, found on the roadside and brought in by customers, were accepted with alacrity. The publican used to take a couple of old carpet bags to the butcher for offal.

George Mitchell and Glen on the moors by the Huntsman

No deliveries could be made to The Traveller's one day because of deep snow. Joel Whiteley, who ran the pub until 1938, sent a laconic note to the brewery: 'Etten up, supp'd up, and b★★★d up. Send me some beer.' The managing director was so taken with the request that he had it framed and hung up in his office.

Around the turn of the century a fiddler played in the pub for customers, long before taped music ousted a livelier way of entertainment. When drinkers had gossiped enough one would call 'Fiddle up, Dick'. His descendants were nicknamed 'Fiddle Up' for decades.

CHAPTER FIVE

THE SINGING SHEPHERD

Composer Haydn Wood, who wrote 'Roses of Picardy' was born at the now demolished Lewisham Hotel situated up Station Road, Slaithwaite. For him and many others, singing seemed to be synonymous with the great outdoors. In 1982, another local, this time a retired shepherd, Arthur Howard, began to find fame as a singing star. Arthur spent most of his life on the Pennine moorlands tending sheep and cattle. Each 5 November and 4 July, American Independence Day, he entertained other shepherds at the Stanhope Arms when the business of the day was over. Arthur was chairman of the Dunford Bridge Shepherds Society for thirty-four years, their meetings held originally at the Millers' Arms, Salters Brook.

Arthur collected over two hundred old songs and recitations. It was Ian Russell, a folklore researcher, who suggested that the shepherd make a record which has now become a treasure trove of almost forgotten songs. The evocative 'A Merry Mountain Child' (the title of the record), 'The Christmas Goose', 'I Bought Three Pigs at Marsden Fair', 'The Farmer's Dog' (that was Piddling Pete) and 'Pace-Egging Song' to name but a few of the one-time favourites brought vividly to life by Arthur's voice.

After the record was released, the 'Singing Shepherd', as he became known, appeared on television's *Look North*, while Yorkshire Television filmed a shepherds meeting, and Arthur in his home surroundings. After that, he regularly sang in public, almost 'bringing the house down' as the saying goes with his version of 'Sucking Pig' rendered at the Castle Museum, York.

One of his friends, Arthur Houps, ex-plate layer on the railway, regaled some of the Stanhope Arms' regulars with tales of how he had gone into a tunnel to retrieve dead sheep. He had

Arthur Howard on a windswept moor near his home

to 'shovel 'em up and put 'em in a sack'. If they were reasonably intact, perhaps merely decapitated, their farmer owner skinned the sheep and boiled the carcasses for his dogs.

The Singing Shepherd's farmhouse was low-beamed and snug, dating back to 1709. He possessed many ancient books, including *Rules of the Shepherds Society* for 1898. One of the rules stated that all Pinders (a term for the men who look after the sheep), owning books of sheep marks, 'If any sheep came into their hands, belonging to any member of the Society shall inform them of, or take them to their respective owners, who shall pay them reasonably for their trouble.' Rule 8 stipulated that each member must attend in person, or send a representative, to each of their respective meetings, or forfeit a shilling each meeting. Sixpence was to be paid for providing dinner, and a further sixpence towards defraying expenses incurred at the meeting. Also, 2s. 6d. were to be collected for each present member's dinner, and surplus monies to cover general expenses of the meeting. Dinner was to be on the table at each meeting at one o'clock. The book also gave detailed descriptions of sheep markings, such as those belonging to Abraham Haigh, of High Gate, Holmbridge, near Holmfirth. 'Branded 8 on near horn, undereaved the near ear, pitched 8 on near side, ruddled over the rump, and down both thighs, and a spot on the head.'

Arthur's father was a founder member of Harden Moss Sheepdog Trials which dated from 1908, and the family had been sheep farmers for generations. There were deeds in the house dating back to 1580.

Before Social Security cushioned unemployment, when navvies were out of work they tramped the roads in search of a job, sometimes earning a few coppers in exchange for a song. Arthur's father once gave a shilling – quite a large amount at the time – to one of those nomads purely for the pleasure of hearing him sing. Arthur enjoyed listening to his father singing and playing on the melodeon, a type of small accordion. Besides entertaining his family, he played for dances at Holme Liberal Club, where he could earn 'three or four bob' for a Saturday evening. In the twenties he was a well-known entertainer at Holmbridge Parish Hall.

Farmers and shepherds used to enjoy driving grouse over the moors from August until December. Arthur and the others thought nothing of walking to the remote Isle of Skye pub, there to regale one another with songs and stories if the weather was too foggy or wet to attend to the grouse.

Saville House Farm, Arthur's old home, is at an elevation of 1,000 feet. His great-grandfather built another farm at Holme, where Arthur was born on Christmas Eve in 1902. One of his songs begins: 'Oh, My Mother said, when I was born, Oh what a present for Christmas morn. . . .'

The top part of the farm was once a weaving shed, housing four handlooms, spinning wheels and twisting frames. One of a family of two boys and four girls, Arthur's early memories were of the big farmhouse kitchen, with its bread reel – two lats of wood suspended from the ceiling – and the smell of freshly baked oatcakes hanging over it to dry. They were delicious spread with butter and treacle. Nearby, by the side of the fireplace, was a rather less pleasant sight, one of his father's belts, used by his mother to chastise her children if they misbehaved.

Arthur Howard, shepherd, at Saville House Farm, Hazlehead

Two sheepdogs, Met and her son, Toss, lived with them. Toss had to be fastened to a table leg so he wouldn't keep running away. One day Arthur was due for 'a belting' and his mother, wearing a long black dress with frighteningly huge leg-o'-mutton sleeves, bore down on her errant son. But she had reckoned without Toss, who loyally sprang to his young master's defence, sinking sharp teeth into one of his mistress's voluminous sleeves, ripping it from top to bottom.

Another early memory was of the time when his young sister dropped a stick over a wall. Arthur thought he had just time enough to retrieve the plaything before two strong calves in the field came to investigate. But his calculations were wrong. Suddenly one charged, pushing its horns beneath his body, sending him soaring back over the wall.

The children attended Holme Board School, a mile away from their farm. Herbert Sydney Warner was the schoolmaster, assisted by a Mrs Bairstow and pupil-teacher Gladys Cartwright. The school roof was of Welsh slates, the yard covered with rolled ashes and clinkers, with bits of grass pushing up between them.

School began with assembly and some hymn singing, then concentration on the 'three Rs'. Those who wished could have singing lessons, but Arthur couldn't be bothered – 'Ah nivver used to tek much notice of music then.' Who would have believed then that it was music that would make him famous?

Christmas was a family affair, the children joining in the pig killing which took place a fortnight before. Arthur and the others were delegated to the gruesome task of holding on to the doomed pigs' tails in the barn until the local butcher had done his work. And how they loved it when the snows of winter arrived, drifts piling so high it was impossible to get to school. Then they could stay cosy in the farmhouse, playing by a big blazing fire.

Arthur's grandma lived at the farm with them until she died, aged ninety-three. On Christmas Eve, stockings were hopefully hung up. Then came the joy of Christmas morning. There was always an onion in each stocking besides the more orthodox orange and apple. One year Arthur grew

Arthur Howard in November 1981

tremendously excited unwrapping a mysterious gift done up with layer after layer of newspaper – no fancy patterned papers then. Lots of string was unknotted, until at long last he arrived at what he was sure, after all that work, would be a 'truly champion' present. His father must have had a warped sense of humour. Lying on the last bit of newspaper was only a burnt bit of cinder. What a disappointment. In the stocking, however, he found a small lead stag with horns, and a lifelike toy pigeon plus the traditional spice pig with a bit of wool for its tail. Then after everyone had compared presents it was time for the children to enjoy their own pig killing, cutting the spice pigs in half, licking until nothing was left but the forlorn little woollen tail.

Even at Christmas visits to relations, or guests going to tea with the Howards, couldn't begin until all the usual farm chores were completed. Then, after a festive meal of spare ribs, everyone sang, recited, or played the piano, according to their various talents. They always finished Christmas Day with a communal sing-song, including 'The Christmas Goose'. On Boxing Day, Arthur would follow the hunt on foot, with Holmfirth, Honley and Meltham hounds, and a huntsman decked out in a green coat.

First the huntsman stood on the moor, blowing his horn. Then, with a tremendous baying, all the hounds were turned loose, ears pricked, making for where the horn was blowing. There was a meet both morning and afternoon, the harriers bent on their duties in pursuit of hares. 'The purpose of the hunt was not to kill off all the foxes and hares, but to hunt for the sheer joy of it,' the Singing Shepherd used to say.

Arthur met his wife Lena when she was nursemaid to the son of a geological surveyor, who had come to the village of Holme to conduct a survey. From then on, according to Arthur, 'It was a natural progression.' As he used to say – 'Tha knows what lads are like when summat fresh comes into a village – all sniffing around.' He wooed and won, and in 1942 the couple moved to Pizenaze Farm at Woodhead, where they ran a thousand sheep on the moor.

In the terrible winter of 1947 half the flock perished, and in the freak snow of April 1981, Arthur's son Rider lost 150 ewes and ewe hoggs, 300 lambs, two cows and two calves. Yet despite the rigours of winter weather and a hard shepherd's life, Arthur Howard wouldn't have changed it 'for owt'. He kept a stalwart belief in country lore, 'If there's ice in November to bear a duck, there'll be nothing after but sludge and muck,' was a favourite saying.

He enjoyed singing in operettas at Holmbridge Parish Hall, appearing in one called *Agatha*. Earlier in life he had worked at Digley Mills, and after putting in a full day there, he recalled how work still awaited him on his return home – milking, haymaking, 'or summat'. In later life his strenuous outdoor work gave way to the less arduous but no less satisfying collecting and performing of the old songs. 'Ah didn't want to spend all me life tied to a cow's tail,' he explained.

The only record he made, *A Merry Mountain Child*, was written by a Holmfirth composer and choirmaster, Joe Perkins, in 1857 or thereabout. What memories its words will always kindle for those Pennine shepherds who attended the meetings where Arthur sang:

Come strike the harp, I long to hear
  Those merry tales of old,
'Ere youth has lost its flowery wreath
  And loving, loving, hearts grown cold.
It brings me back those happy times,
  When roving free and wild,
I played about my native home
  I played about my native home,
  I played about my native home –
A merry mountain child.

But the twinkle in the Singing Shepherd's eye was never more evident than in his rendering of the rather more earthy 'Muck Spreader'. Here are some sample verses:

Down on our farm we are quite up to date,
And mechanisation a by word of late,
For every task there's a gadget to match,
And our muck spreader's the best of the batch.
  Fling it here, fling it there,
  And if you're standing by
  You'll all get your share.
The parson his windows were all open wide,
A generous helping descended inside,
The parson at table intoned, 'Let us pray,'
When the manure from Heaven came flying his way.
  [Chorus] Fling it here, fling it there etc.

Singing shepherd Arthur Howard went to his last Merry Mountain in August 1982.

CHAPTER SIX

A COUNTRY SHOW

Few days out are as pleasant as those spent at a country show. But for those who need to be within striking distance of a public convenience, hour after hour spent watching dogs and sheep at Harden Moss can be more of a torment than a pleasure. Especially if you're a lady. Doris, a mill worker, was among crowds at Harden Moss one year and eventually needed to enter one of those makeshift, uninviting chemical toilets. So unsavoury was the atmosphere that she almost vomited – her false teeth shot straight out into the gaping, awful aperture.

Flustered, poor Doris re-emerged, to ask her friend if she had a match. 'Why, have you started smoking?' Hilda wanted to know, handing her a Bryant and May's. Doris snatched it and disappeared again, looking like a female Valentino, a handkerchief swathed across her face to act as a mask. After some minutes out she came again, red faced but triumphant, false teeth bundled in the handkerchief.

'They'll be alright once I've doused 'em in Dettol at home,' she explained. Ever after that eventful day, Doris only had to smile for Hilda to be reminded of that particular sheep dog trials at Harden Moss, when it wasn't only the sheep who were sorely tried.

Trials and tribulations, large and small, are part and parcel of country living – but looked back on as 'the happiest days of our lives' by those who endured them.

Jenny Wortley, born 1908, lived in White Lea, a farmhouse at the top end of Standedge. Her Dad, George William, was a teamer, delivering coal and groceries for a place down in Marsden. They had two horses for negotiating steep hills. Marmaduke, 'Duke' for short, was a shire horse with a white

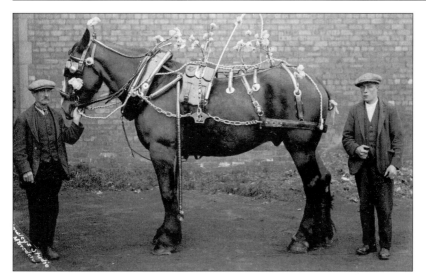

Mr Wortley and one of his 'hosses'

patch on his forehead. Big and strong he may have been, but he couldn't face hills. One morning he stopped dead in his tracks, so the teamer had to swap horses, putting the other carthorse in the shafts. That one never stopped until he reached the summit. Coal wasn't bagged, but shunted outside on the pavement. With seven in the Wortley household, there were plenty to shovel it inside.

Jenny recalls the feel of cold lino on stone floors, and how they dreaded getting out of their warm bed in the depths of winter to fumble for the 'jerry' beneath the bed. They only had plain white chamber pots at first, later acquiring a finer one for 'a bob' decorated with roses on the outside. Even that seemingly mundane operation had its hazards at times – once Jenny sat on one, and it cracked. Her mother nearly had a heart attack, wondering who had suffered most, child or chamber pot.

They had an outside privy with newspaper squares hanging from a nail on the wall. When the men came round to clean it out, the children would shout, 'Hey up – t' marmalade cart's coming' as it came into sight. What a good job the chaps who came to empty them never went on strike. The blessings of modern plumbing and sanitation were undreamt of luxuries for ordinary Pennine folk at the turn of the century.

Another, rather more pleasant, regular caller was the milkman. If nobody was at home, a jug was left on doorsteps with a plate to cover the milk when he called. If they forgot to leave one, the milkman went in and found it. This wasn't a problem in those days as doors were never locked. There was nothing to pinch in any case.

To brighten the house up Mrs Wortley scoured the hearth with red ruddle, and used a cream-coloured Donkey stone with an imprint of a donkey to scour the stone sink. Scouring doorsteps in preparation for the weekend was a matter of the utmost pride to Pennine housewives. Inside, folk were equally houseproud and set great store on keeping surfaces and furniture polished and clean. Old black woollen stockings covered polished table legs to stop them being scuffed with clogs, and there was a block of blacklead specially for cleaning the Yorkshire range. Jenny remembers having a mauve velvet frock when she was a child, bought from Marsden Co-op. When she outgrew it, her mother, Annie, cut it into squares and used them for blackleading the fireplace. Fells naptha soap was for washing greasy overalls, white Windsor soap for faces.

Discipline in school kept children 'toeing the line'. Jenny's brother, Joseph William, was caught sucking a sweet in class one day, a seemingly minor infringement. The headmaster put him over a desk and thrashed him with a long, swishing cane. When Joe complained to his father he received no sympathy. Boys were expected to be tough.

'If tha does owt wrong again, ah hope he puts thi ovver t' desk again tomorrer,' was the response. On another occasion, Ivy, one of the daughters, had been talking during lessons. As a punishment the teacher stuck a plaster across her mouth. At dinnertime Ivy ran home in tears. That was too much for her mother, whose heart was much softer than her husband's. Though still 'in her muck', wearing a grey check apron with a harding sackcloth one on top, she exploded, 'Tha can tell yon teacher ah'm coming to see her.'

As good as her word, that afternoon Mrs Wortley clattered purposefully to the school in her clogs, sleeves rolled up at the elbows. There were thirty-six steps to climb, and a sign that read 'Please ring the bell'. The irate mother ignored the bell, storming straight into the classroom. 'You put plaster on my daughter's mouth,' she thundered. 'Do you know what I'd have done if I'd seen you doing it – ah'd have tekken it off and clapped it on thine!' Ivy spasmodically suffered from fits, 'How would you have gone on if she'd had a fit?' demanded Mrs Wortley of the by this time cringing teacher. In her defence, the teacher asked the child's mother how she would go on with forty-two in a class. 'If I'd a *hundred* and forty-two I wouldn't stick plaster over a mouth,' Mrs Wortley countered unabashed.

Next week the repentant teacher made Ivy a monitor, and 'took her under her wing'. When the child did have a fit, the family's remedy was to throw cold water in her face, and the doctor assured them that Ivy would grow out of it. When she had a very bad fit, the doctor predicted it would be her last. And it was. She had indeed 'grown out of them'.

When children were late the headmaster pulled their socks down and cracked their legs. Jenny's father told them, 'Tha mun up wi' thi clog and catch him one.' He wasn't always on the side of officialdom. But it was easier said than done. Sometimes there were half a dozen or more woe-begone looking children standing all in a row, their legs red and sore.

Mrs Wortley used to buy a stone of flour from the Co-op. Sometimes the manager happened to be giving away damaged apples, they were a godsend. They could be turned into delicious apple pies, or apple sauce to go with a bit of pork.

Mr Wortley went to the stables every evening around 10 p.m. to make sure the horses were alright. If one was 'out of sorts' he stayed up all night with it, sitting on an old box covered with straw.

Once one of the Wortley boys bought a paraffin lamp for his parents. It wasn't two minutes before his father blew it out. 'It takes too much to run that thing, we'll light a candle,' he decided. Although he never spared himself, he was loathe to waste money or resources. He could, according to Jenny, 'wash himself in an egg cup full of water!'

Rather than pay a chimney sweep he threw 'spewers' – oven squibs – into the fire, where they cracked and banged like mad. 'Tha gonna blow all t' fixtures out, Willie,' remonstrated his missus.

'My father was always agate [busy] setting t' chimney on fire,

Jenny Ellison (née Wortley), 1984

using straw many a time,' remembered Jenny. 'We hardly dare leave him in t' house.'

But William didn't care a hang as long as the fire got going and bread baking. It was worth it, though – the hot oven enabled his wife to bake parkin 'a foot thick' for Bonfire Day. Replete with roast potatoes, treacle toffee and a slice of foot-thick parkin, the children roamed the district singing their bonfire song:

> We've come a cop coiling, for Bonfire Night,
> We'll eat nowt, nor steal nowt,
> But bid you goodnight,
> Fol de de, foldidi,
> Foldididdle di do day.

Gleefully the children blacked their faces, donned old long dresses and shawls, and then raced off, carrying an empty cocoa tin for a collecting box. If the pangs of hunger assailed them, back they scampered into the kitchen to grab another wedge of parkin, shove it up their jumpers, and dash outside again. What consternation when someone put a jumping jack underneath the front door! Never mind that the excitement of Bonfire Night was over, soon it would be time to be thinking about Christmas.

And there were other pleasures for the children. Cadging butter tubs from grocers, taking the hoops from the middles and making crêpe paper coloured flyballs to festoon them with. Playing out on dark evenings was fun, too. The children delighted in opening a shop door, yelling 'A penn'orth o' kick me over t' counter drops, Mister,' then racing off under cover of pitch darkness, the shopkeeper's irate bellowing echoing in their ears.

Sometimes, on frosty nights, Jenny loved to slide down hillsides on a cardboard box, getting her navy knickers 'frozen through'. 'Ah'll see tha has a proper sledge, lass,' her Dad promised, contriving one from an ancient iron bedstead with the luxury of a piece of potato sacking tied across with string. It was marvellous! Jenny and her friends were allowed to play outside until the church bells pealed. Then, if they didn't return home at once, they received 'a clout across t' earhole' when they did.

One year, coming up to Christmas, Mrs Wortley suggested buying a bit of carpet. She'd seen some going cheap in a sale and thought it would go well at home. Inside the farmhouse was only a bit of potato sacking by the door to wipe muddy clogs and boots on, and a big pegged rug before the fire.

'Nay, lass, what thi' talking about? We ain't worn t' flags through yet,' her husband admonished. 'Be reasonable!' And that was that.

The bedrooms had stone floors, covered with lino, and whitewashed walls. Water was drawn from an old iron tank outside the house. Best of all, from a child's point of view, there was a huge open hearth with a wide chimney, wide enough for the plumpest Father Christmas to wriggle down once the fire was out.

One Christmas Eve, during the First World War, William bent low and bellowed, 'Allo Santa, lad, atta thear?' for the benefit of Jenny and the others.

''As ter yerd owt, Dad?' she asked with bated breath.

'Nooa, ah ain't. He's waiting till tha's fast asleep,' came the pragmatic reply.

After Father Christmas had gone to all the bother of squeezing down the chimney there were only simple little presents in Jenny's long black woollen stocking hanging over her bed. Lucky bags, containing a tiny toy or ring, were pounced on with glee. Often there were a 'pennorth o' monkey nuts' and an orange, apple and new penny. Rag dolls that were absolutely marvellous, tinged with a magical aura, especially as they weren't exactly ten a penny in the shops. They were unique. Unknown to the little girl, they had come into being while her mother stitched away in the long winter evenings after the rest of the family were in bed. Then there was the sugar pig, and for the girls, a big bag each full of coloured glass beads which, later that happy morning, they strung into gaudy necklaces and bracelets. Sometimes there were slates, packets of chalk, pretend sweet cigarettes – maybe a chocolate cigar – and marbles for the boys or exercise books to write stories in. One year Jenny found a bright red pillar box to put her Saturday pennies in with a bright new penny rattling inside, humble beginnings to start her off on the road to riches! Oh, the machinations that had to be gone through to try and extricate those coins, once they disappeared inside! How many frustrating hours were wasted prodding and poking with an old knife in a vain attempt to get the coin to position itself correctly.

At that time of year festive aromas, the baking of cakes and puddings mingled with other wintry scents. If a member of the family had bronchitis, a tallow candle was lit and the juice dripped on to a sheet of brown paper and clamped on to the patient's chest.

Mr Wortley set traps for rabbits, 'Always a cheap, tasty meal.' 'But our bloomin' cat got caught in one, and had to be carried, still with it's leg in the trap, to the blacksmith to be set free,' Jenny recalls. Pussy roamed the locality on three legs after that misfortune.

With sentiments none so different from Mr Wortley's, the local doctor believed in prescribing a bit of wisdom in preference to expensive drugs, giving his patients 'a good talking to'.

'Can tha gie me owt for t' wind doctor?' an elderly chap pleaded one raw winter evening.

'Aye, lad,' gravely replied the medical man, knowing his patient's propensity for mushy peas and chips washed down with gallons of ale. 'Go buy a kite, and don't follow it into the pub,' was his advice.

To treat a wicklow, villagers waited until a cow was 'ready to go' then placed part of the warm cowclap on to the affected finger or thumb, securing it with a bit of bandage or old sheeting. Marshmallow ointment was kept in most homes for drawing out 'barbs' or spells; if none was available, soap and white sugar mixed together were used. And in a precaution that had nothing to do with science but everything with superstition, newly born babies on the hill farms had big binders wrapped round their bodies to 'hold them together'.

Pennine children didn't need many bought toys when they had all the freedom of the great outdoors. What better summer holiday could there be than playing in a stream, leaping from one stepping stone to another, dress pushed into navy knickers to keep it from getting wet. Catching tadpoles, sailing paper boats – waiting for jam-jars to be emptied so they could be returned to the shop, getting a halfpenny for a pound size jar. Once, an assistant tried to fob Jenny off with a Dolly Blue instead, but Jenny stood her ground for the cash.

William Wortley's working garb consisted of old trousers, shirt and waistcoat, a potato sack flung round his shoulders, and bits of sacking tied round his legs, secured with string. Equally unconcerned with domestic appearances, he didn't agree with having even coconut matting on the floor, arguing that 'we don't want bits o' muck ligging in between that damned stuff'. But with oil lamps glowing in the winter time they were 'right happy', playing ludo and snakes and ladders, the light from the lamp casting a rosy glow when snow lay deep and crisp and even on the hills and fields outside.

The family did possess a gramophone with a big horn. Having no conception of how it worked, the children thought that little people lived inside it, producing lovely music that soared up through that horn: 'Poet and Peasant Overture', 'Stars and Stripes' and 'Under the Double Eagle'. When one of the records cracked, Wortley sniffed, 'Aye, it's not the only thing that's cracked.'

Sometimes one of them went to the 'chip oile' to get fish and chips to round off the evening. 'Tha can't work off chips and fish, but ah'll 'ave 'em for me supper,' Jenny's Dad used to say. They took a white pot basin, returning with it full of chips covered over with paper, and fish wrapped in newspaper. Jenny's mother doled them out by hand, 'Salt, pepper and vinegar were knocking about on't table' and 'ee, we were happy!'

Between nine and ten in the evening William could usually be found in the Red Lion down in Marsden, 'telling t' tale'.

Up in the farmhouse was a long table, which was scrubbed every day with either Vim or Panshine. On Sundays it sported a white starched tablecloth. Ham shanks were frequently on the menu, boiled up in a big black iron pan with lots of mushy peas. On the rare occasions he went shopping, William, who considered it 'cissy' for men to carry a basket, took an old pillow case instead, 'Put a stone of flour in this, lad,' he would say. A potato sack served for any other stuff he might buy. Sometimes blood from meat oozed through on to its wrapping paper. 'Makes no difference, it all goes down t' same hole,' was the teamer's game attitude.

Mr and Mrs Wortley always treated themselves to Marsden Electric Theatre every Thursday; it was their one night out. Here they were transported to a world far removed from their Pennine home, watching film stars Mary Pickford, cowboy Tom Mix, and performers like Jackie Coogan – once they even saw Houdini.

Jenny and her friends went to Marsden to the pictures on Saturdays, where they sat in the front row, stamping their feet and making more din than the matinée itself – high spirits which only contributed to the enjoyment. Letting their hair down, they would throw monkey nut shells and bits of screwed up toffee paper to attract the attention of their chums.

A cobbler at the Co-op put irons on clogs, which lasted about a month. Some people had boots made into clogs. Then there was a shop in Marsden that provided the quaint but useful service of knitting new 'feet' on woollen stockings, besides plying their main trade of selling confectionery. William favoured a mingled shade of wool socks, predominantly dark red, 'right thick ribbed'. As for Mrs Wortley, she wore fine cashmere stockings. Stockings and other garments needed continuous repair and she was always 'agate' (busy) with the wooden mushroom mending and darning.

In 1921 Jenny left school aged thirteen and began working in a mill, though employees weren't allowed to go near machinery until they were fourteen. Jenny earned 11s. 4d. a week at first, working from half past seven in the morning until five in the evening, with an hour off for dinner. She gave all her wage to her mother for her keep, and she was handed back 'a bob a week spending brass'. In those days a big joint of meat could be bought for 5 shillings.

There were fourteen girls working in the winding department, including Jenny. If they needed a brief rest, there was a basket of bobbins to perch on. All wore black Italian cloth overalls, black woollen stockings, and clogs. When the 'Gaffer' nipped out for a brew up or to the 'lav' the winders grabbed the opportunity of a respite from their work and had a sing-song and bit of a dance. Among their favourite tunes was 'There is a happy land, Far, far away, Where Saints in glory stand, Far, far away.' Perhaps the longing in those words is a reflection of the relatively hard lives the mill girls endured.

Joe, Jenny's brother, joined the Territorials in 1924, at 'Slowit' (Slaithwaite) Drill Hall. Excited at the prospect of his new venture, every time Joe was on a tram he sang 'Ding dong, we're off!' in high glee. Jenny and Ivy went with him to register. An officer asked, 'Havn't you two had something to eat?' But they couldn't afford a cup of coffee, let alone a sandwich. Seeing how things stood, the kindly officer ordered, 'Make sure these youngsters have something to eat.' Afterwards all three walked home from Slaithwaite to Marsden, linking arms and singing joyfully on that moonlit night, 'happy as larks'.

Meetings between the sexes reflected the generally tough attitude to life. Boys didn't 'go down on their knees' to ask a girl out, even 'umming and aahing' when it came to paying to go inside the cinema. 'And it was nobbut fourpence,' remembers Jenny.

Her first romantic encounter was an outing to the pictures with her friend Florence and a couple of local lads. When there was a seemingly unaccountable delay at the pay box, Florence, realizing what was amiss, said, 'Come on, lass, it looks as though we'll have to stand our own corner.' Once the girls had paid for themselves, the youths shambled in after them, somewhat shamefaced.

At one point in his life William worked at the railway station. It was then that the family enjoyed their first excursion, to New Brighton. Assisted travel was one of the perks of his employment – he went free, his wife at half fare, the children at only a quarter of the full fare. They went for a whole week in 1920.

Paddling in the sea, Jenny and Ivy pushed their dresses inside their navy blue week-day knickers, convenient items with pockets on one side for hankies. White knickers were for weekends only. During the day the girls wore checked gingham dresses and pumps. Jenny recalls how, when their parents went out for a drink in the evening, they were put to bed in the lodging house. It was to be their one and only holiday.

Back home again, William started keeping rabbits in the big coal 'hole', sometimes swapping them for Bantam hens. Although he could never bring himself to eat one of his own rabbits, if Annie bought a wild one from the shop he'd no scruples about eating that. Yet he could screw a hen's neck round 'without batting an eyelid'.

On Sundays the family went to Marsden Spiritualist Church, where on chilly days a stove in the middle of the room warmed the place up a bit. Jenny loved to sing, 'We're marching to Zion, beautiful, beautiful Zion, We're marching to Zion, the beautiful city of God.' She remembers how prizes were awarded to children who attended for a whole year.

After each service the family went home where best clothes were removed, and second best put on until it was time to return to church for the next service. They attended three times on the Sabbath. Nor was religious observance confined to church-going. At home grace was said before and after every meal. If any member of the family forgot, William beckoned the culprit to return to the table. 'Hoi, tha come back. Tha's not said "Thank thee God, for what ah've received".'

During the 1926 General Strike, when times were bad, many were forced to take bowls along to the soup kitchen which was organized in the Socialist Club. There they were filled with hot, nourishing stews made from bones, carrots, potatoes, turnips and any other cheap ingredients and handed back to the grateful recipients.

But the good times outnumbered the bad. Every May Day William Wortley showed his big black shire horse, grooming it to perfection and staying up with it through the night to make sure that it didn't lie down and get dirty. It's feet were specially washed, using a bucket of soapy water, the bit in its mouth scrupulously cleaned. The horse looked 'a real treat' on the big day, with gleaming brasses, harness, and pink and white carnations woven among them for additional finery. Jenny helped by making pom-poms with a cardboard template, pulling

Pat Ellison, Jenny's daughter, who was
picked as 'Miss Marsden'

the green and pink wool through the hole in the centre to make
a contrast with the shining black horse.

If his horse won, William was either rewarded with a cash
prize or bottle of whisky. Either way, there'd be nothing left
when he returned home, only the rosette on his horse to prove
that it had been placed.

At Marsden and Slaithwaite Carnival, held every June or July,
the Co-op, Johnson's, and Hanson's the haulage firm each had a
decorated float. Truly, a highlight of the Pennine year. Jenny's
daughter, Pat, was crowned 'Miss Marsden' one year to her
mother's great delight.

CHAPTER SEVEN

OLD MOORE – HIS GRANDDAUGHTER REMEMBERS

Even the poorest families didn't like to be without a copy of *Old Moore's Almanack*, to foretell probable future prospects. From its pages they hoped to glean some indication as to the weather for the coming year, and any other portents that might affect their fortunes. Few knew, or cared, who the compiler of their almanack was.

Albert Walker took over the mantle of Yorkshire's seer from his father, William, who began a printing works in Otley in 1811, which became a limited company in 1904. Eventually, the enterprise grew to include ownership of a group of newspapers consisting of the *Wharfedale and Airedale Observer*, the *Ilkley Free Press and Gazette*, and the *Shipley Times and Express*.

Apart from 'watching the stars' and reading people's bumps (shape of their heads), Albert was also known as 'The Whistling Commercial' because, besides having a talent for writing, he was an entertainer who whistled happy tunes. Giving monologues and recitations was one of his hobbies. He wrote a book, *The Road*, describing life as a commercial traveller in the early years of the century. It opens with this verse:

> Give me the road! Where true bliss you may find,
> An order book full, and a purse well lined.
> Good cheer, good friends, a good inn your abode.
> Then hip, hip, hooray! for the road, the road!

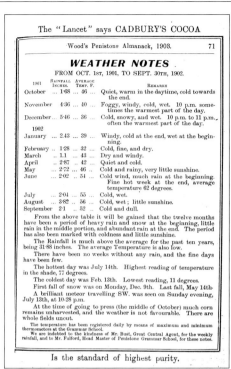

The *"Lancet"* says CADBURY'S COCOA

Wood's Penistone Almanack, 1903.   71

WEATHER NOTES

FROM OCT. 1st, 1901, TO SEPT. 30TH, 1902.

1901	RAINFALL INCHES.	AVERAGE TEMP. F.	REMARKS
October	1·68	46	Quiet, warm in the daytime, cold towards the end.
November	4·36	40	Foggy, windy, cold, wet. 10 p.m. sometimes the warmest part of the day.
December	5·46	36	Cold, snowy, and wet. 10 p.m. to 11 p.m. often the warmest part of the day.
1902			
January	2·43	39	Windy, cold at the end, wet at the beginning.
February	1·28	32	Cold, fine, and dry.
March	1.1	43	Dry and windy.
April	2·87	42	Quiet and cold.
May	2·72	46	Cold and rainy, very little sunshine.
June	2·02	54	Cold wind, much rain at the beginning. Fine hot week at the end, average temperature 62 degrees.
July	2·04	55	Cold, wet.
August	3·82	56	Cold, wet ; little sunshine.
September	2·1	52	Cold and dull.

From the above table it will be gained that the twelve months have been a period of heavy rain and snow at the beginning, little rain in the middle portion, and abundant rain at the end. The period has also been marked with coldness and little sunshine.

The Rainfall is much above the average for the past ten years, being 31·88 inches. The average Temperature is also low.

There have been no weeks without any rain, and the fine days have been few.

The hottest day was July 14th. Highest reading of temperature in the shade, 77 degrees.

The coldest day was Feb. 13th. Lowest reading, 11 degrees.

First fall of snow was on Monday, Dec. 9th. Last fall, May 14th.

A brilliant meteor travelling SW. was seen on Sunday evening, July 13th, at 10·28 p.m.

At the time of going to press (the middle of October) much corn remains unharvested, and the weather is not favourable. There are whole fields uncut.

The temperature has been registered daily by means of maximum and minimum thermometers at the Grammar School.

We are indebted to the kindness of Mr. Bust, Great Central Agent, for the weekly rainfall, and to Mr. Fulford, Head Master of Penistone Grammar School, for these notes.

Is the standard of highest purity.

Weather Notes from the 1903 *Almanack*

Chapters include such highlights as 'Our Amusements', with the following description of diversions on the road. 'Chaffing the barmaid, having a quiet flirtation with her is a favourite source of amusement to the dawdling commercial who has not brains above petticoats, a neat figure, and an immense chignon.' Another, entitled 'Our Improvidence', has this to say about his fellow travellers: 'You see us then in all the glory of sealskin waistcoats, also tobacco pouches, cigar cases, fuzee-boxes of the same material.' One chapter concerns habitual grumblers, another the sick commercial, and what characteristics are desirable in a traveller: quickness and rapidity should be part of the model traveller's abilities. A good appearance is equally to be desired in a representative, for a shuffling gait, a seedy suit of clothes, a dirty paper collar and front would not advance you in the esteem of the man before whom you stood. A pair of bleary eyes and couple of dirty hands are equally undesirable. A shabby

Albert Walker, Yorkshire's 'Old Moore'

hat might lose you an order, for in many cases the buyer judges that the poor quality of your attire reflects the fact you travel for an unimportant firm, that can't afford to pay you well. Good health is really indispensable – an ailing man should never go out on the road.

Albert described their sample cases, too, noting, among others, that gentlemanly individual, with two neat brown paper parcels, both of them laced tight with strong whipcord twine. We may be almost sure they mean groceries, dried fruit, and the like. Ten to one, the traveller with iron-bound sample cases of the strongest sheet tin is dealing in ironmongery of some description.

'Our Waitress' was another important personage in the commercial's life. 'Her morning attire – that which she adopts up to the dinner hour, is a clean cotton print, fashionably made. By dinner time, a nice merino of maroon, or other quiet colour, decked out with bows, ruches, panniers and tucks set off her trim figure.' He tells how one of his chums made a bet that a certain waitress would be ready with a reply to anything. The bet was made, the gas turned off, and commercial James stuck a candle in his mouth (with proper protection from the grease!). Then, as soon as the other end of the candle had been lighted, Lizzie was duly summoned.

'Will you please extinguish the light?' James managed to stutter.

'Oh, yes, Sir, with the greatest pleasure. I see you always carry a brass extinguisher on your face,' said Lizzie boldly but with perfect civility, as she pulled away the candle and stuck the lighted end in the mouth of the 'candlestick'.

Besides publishing *The Road*, other works by Old Moore were *The Sting of the Adder; A Tale of Thrilling Interest, Tales You Should Read* and *The Rose of Wharfedale – A Tale of Great Interest.*

There is one particularly amusing incident recalled by his granddaughter, Marjorie Alberta, from when she was a child. One day one of his workers dashed into Albert's office and asked, 'What shall I put for the weather, Mr Walker, on 20 June?'

'Dammit, man,' snorted the Boss, 'put snow.' Albert sprang from a family who forged ahead by brains and initiative, they couldn't abide 'gormlessness'. Indeed, his father, William, had started the business with very limited capital, and when trade grew enough to rely on the use of machinery, he used his ingenuity and invented it himself. Both father and son were commercially minded.

Advertised on the back of *The Road*, then obtainable from Victoria Works, Otley, was the new *Sunday School Register* 'which will last 2½ years, and secures an absolutely accurate and very easily kept record of your class attendance. Sample copy, post free, 4½d., or 12 copies, post free, for 3/–. Plus *Walkers Golden Reciter* – A choice collection of ancient and modern pieces by the best authors. In ornamental cloth cover, post free, 1/3d. Also, *The Reciters Treasury of Temperance Pieces*. A choice selection of new and original readings, recitations and dialogues, neatly bound in cloth, gilt lettered, post free, 1/2d.'

Marjorie in Grandpa Old Moore's
garden at Otley in 1921

Old Moore and his wife Jane had two sons and three
daughters, one of whom was Lily, destined to become Marjorie
Alberta's mother. At the Otley Works, children's toy books were
also published. At the stationer's shop on Kirkgate a huge
machine powered the lights in the offices. A brass plaque had the
name 'Albert' inscribed on it. He died in 1923, leaving his
beloved granddaughter an album of photographs of herself. A
keen amateur photographer, Old Moore had photographed
Marjorie every year on her birthday, taking the first picture on
20 July 1907, when he was sixty-eight. The final portrait was
taken in 1922 when he was eighty-three and Marjorie sixteen.
His grave is in Otley cemetery.

His granddaughter was his pride and joy. He made toys for
her, having the magic of an Edwardian Christmas at his
fingertips, a talent he passed on to daughter Lily, Marjorie's
mother. One year there was a deftly hand-made circular
mahogany board, with divisions all the way round with fortunes
and character readings inscribed on them, the whole overlooked
by a witch-like figure cunningly contrived to hold a long stick in
her hand. She was spun round, and when she stopped, her

pointer indicated one's character, or gave a warning. One stricture noted, 'You are contemplating something naughty – do not do it.' Marjorie kept the Wheel of Fortune all her life, still pausing for thought before embarking on some undignified pursuit if the pointer spun to a warning. While Old Moore had printed in one section the sobering words, 'You definitely must beware of vanity, it is contemptible,' other predictions were more to Marjorie's liking, such as 'You will wed and be blissfully happy.'

Unlike so many children of her era living in the Pennines, Marjorie's family was relatively well to do. Her father, Frederick Holroyd, owned the Yorkshire Die Stamping Co. Ltd, Relief Works, Trafalgar Street, Bradford, so Christmas time for Marjorie as a child was wonderful.

One year Old Moore, her Grandpa, asked a local joiner to make a Noah's Ark for his little pet. It was a beautiful work of craftsmanship with a roof of brown tiles, and all the animals

Marjorie Motley at her Pateley Bridge home in 1982, surrounded by some of her childhood games

carved from the same cream-coloured wood. There was even a little ladder for them to 'walk up' into the Ark. Figures of Noah and his wife stood at the entrance and a small white dove bearing an olive branch in its mouth was perched on top. Another Christmas Grandpa bought a 3 feet tall silver-grey teddy bear for his beloved granddaughter. It had been one of the bears featured in the show, *The Teddy Bears Picnic* at the Queen's Theatre, Otley. Marjorie Alberta had been taken to see a performance and had fallen in love with the bear.

Then there was the time she was given the gorgeous 24 inch high China doll, complete with long golden hair, eyelashes and blue eyes which closed when she was put to bed. Oh, what lovely clothes she had, all hand-made by Marjorie's mother. A beautifully stitched Red Riding Hood cloak was made to go over a pink satin dress resplendent with diamanté buttons down the front, and a wide sash to tie at the back. And underneath a delicately stitched petticoat and knickers to match. The height of elegance, Dolly's dress had a lace collar and cuffs – and a local cobbler had even been called upon by Grandpa Old Moore to make the doll a pair of black patent leather shoes. Nothing was too good for the lucky Marjorie Alberta.

Dolly's morning dress was of crisp blue and white gingham. For outings she had a black satin coat with shiny black buttons and white lace collar and cuffs. Dolly Holroyd was so high-class she even possessed a specially made trunk to keep her outfits in! It had an elegant curved lid and was enamelled pale blue, with smart gold bands encircling it. Inside was a tray, bearing a doll-sized piece of soap and tiny towel.

Such delights could never be duplicated in shops – only Santa Claus could have brought them, Marjorie Alberta knew without a doubt. When she grew older, Marjorie received a gilt-edged autograph album. In 1922, a friend wrote inside, 'Be what you are, Do what you can, You can shine like a glow worm, If you cannot be a star.' And who could deny the wisdom of 'A frown stretches from ear to ear, but a smile is immeasurable.'

A button hook, with a string attached, was another useful if less magical gift she received in the twenties. Marjorie realized that dresses with stupid zips up the back were at last manageable!

Besides enjoying a privileged childhood, she also went to

Greystones Boarding School for Girls, at Goathland, near Whitby. Her cousin Marguerite accompanied her as they set out for the steam train which would take them from Otley Station in the September of 1918, as the Great War drew to its close. Both girls had with them big wicker baskets and a tin trunk each. The porter who carried them for 'the young ladies' was Albert Modley, later to become famous as a Northern comedian.

As the train began to move out of the station, Marjorie's mother began to cry. But her daughter, with a new and independent life beckoning at the other end of the journey, waved her hankie, calling out in a jolly voice, 'Goodbye, Mother – Don't worry about me.'

Greystones was a select establishment; the fees were £50 a term, and thirty-five girls, all between the ages of twelve and sixteen, boarded. Their uniforms were made by the local dressmaker; summer costumes were of oatmeal-coloured tussore silk, worn with a white silk blouse on Sundays for attendance at church. Panama hats shaded their brows on summer days. White lawn or cotton knickers were *de rigueur*, while navy knickers with a pocket at one side for a handker-chief were worn over combinations in winter. The girls wore garters that suspended black woollen stockings, while their calf-length gym slips were made from Black Watch tartan, with black girdles slung round the hips. Winter blouses were of a green Viyella-type material.

On arriving at Greystones, the cousins were shown up to a bedroom containing two beds. This was privileged accommo-dation; the majority of the girls slept in dormitories. Oilcloth covered the floor, there were two bedside lockers and a white candle in each holder. A rug placed at each bedside took off the floor's chill. Plain white chamber pots resided beneath the beds. Their room also contained a big white pottery bowl and jug for washing which was filled with hot water each morning by Fanny, the housekeeper. There was a pottery soap dish and two toothbrush holders.

'We had to take our own towels, marked with our names, just as every other personal possession had to be marked,' remembered Marjorie. Their mothers used to buy thick Turkish towelling by the yard for the girls' periods and these makeshift sanitary towels were put into a slop pail after use. A far cry from the discreet, disposable protection now available.

The school provided white cotton sheets and two blankets for each girl. Marjorie had a blue eiderdown, blue slippers and matching dressing-gown. Marguerite preferred pink.

The principal, Miss Girling, wore a pince-nez on a gold chain, and black satin high-necked blouses with velvet ribbon through the neckline openings. Marjorie recalls how the skirts of the mistresses were a demure ankle-length, and how the mistress, Miss Owen, had fashionably 'draped' twin curtains of dark hair over each cheek bone.

The school matron was attired in a nurse's uniform. Her hair was braided in plaits, then coiled into two earphones, smack over the ears. 'Goodness knows how she ever heard what was going on!' Marjorie wondered.

A number of girls from down south boarded at Greystones, and they thought themselves quite superior to the 'Yorkshire lasses'. They pronounced class as 'clarse', similarly enunciating bath. One day one of these proud creatures called Marjorie 'common', and poor Marjorie slunk off into a corner to cry, her face burning with a mixture of shame and anger.

'Well, if you know how Albert Modley talked then, you know how I talked. I could have been his female counterpart,' she once said.

After that incident her parents decided she ought to have elocution lessons, just as some girls took singing or piano lessons, at extra cost.

Sport figured high on the curriculum. A neighbouring riding school was available for Saturday morning lessons and Wednesday afternoons were dedicated to hockey or tennis. Marguerite, who had already been tutored to 'speak posh' took singing lessons.

At mealtimes, a big brass gong summoned pupils to the large dining hall. For breakfast there was a choice between boiled or poached eggs, followed by either syrup or honey. The honey came from the bees on the surrounding moors and was quite delicious.

At Greystones etiquette was as important as academic pursuits, so if a girl ended up with sticky fingers after eating bread and honey, she was in trouble. Only teachers were allowed to have marmalade instead.

One summer evening, Marjorie and Marquerite decided to have a picnic in their bedroom, and invited another girl to share the feast. They had bought a huge tin of peaches and some big bars of milk chocolate with money sent by their parents. They realized they had no tin opener, but dear Fanny came to the rescue. She was persuaded to sneak one up from the kitchen, from where she also produced some dessert spoons.

The peaches were tipped into the huge wash bowl, then all the girls dipped in together. Any 'tuck' was supposed to be handed in, and kept in a special cupboard, but the cousins used to keep supplies of their favourite milk chocolate hidden beneath the mattresses.

After the feast they threw the empty tin out of the window. Early next morning they were in a state of panic when they heard the farmer and his horse arriving at 6.00 a.m. to cut the hay. The tin! Marjorie shot out of bed, dashed downstairs in her nightie to retrieve it, and put it in the litter bin, where it ought to have been disposed of in the first place. Nicely brought up young ladies don't simply whizz empty tins out of bedroom windows, do they. . . ?

Misbehaviour was punished by 'lines', not by corporal methods. If a girl had to write, say, 'I have been untidy' a hundred times, it was almost certain that she would not be in a hurry to commit a similar misdemeanour again.

Marguerite's great failing was boys, and she flirted with the farmer's lads whenever the opportunity arose. Yet, ironically, she was the one who never married.

In her later years Marjorie became what was known as a 'stage door Johnnie', a rather more modest version of the modern-day fan. Owning a house in Scarborough as well as Pateley Bridge, she delighted in writing to artistes such as Ken Dodd, and would wait for ages to have a word with the famous after their performance. She never forgot Grandpa Old Moore though, however many celebrities and exciting new faces she encountered.

But no grown-up pleasures can surpass the ones of childhood, and Marjorie Alberta, even in her seventies, recollected those Christmas toys. They included the toy shop, over 2 feet long, with its miniature drawers containing tea, coffee, and other

The same Brussels lace collar, which was once worn by Albert Walker's wife Jane, now adorns a 1939 teddy bear

commodities and a wooden counter complete with miniature scales, and tiny paper bags to hold customers' requirements. Green cupboards were beneath the counter, and on top small glass jars filled with tiny dolly mixtures and 'cherry lips'. The quality of such toys meant that they lasted for years, and gave a lifetime's enjoyment.

Old Moore must have retained that essential spirit of childhood himself throughout his life, for when he visited his Fleet Street office he took a whopping big teddy bear home for his wife Jane, whom he had married on 24 July 1865 at South Hackney in London. Only later did they live in Ashfield Place, Otley. In the archives of Otley Museum can still be seen memorabilia of Albert Walker, Old Moore, of *Almanack* fame.

CHAPTER EIGHT

THE CHRISTMAS BEAR – ADA TRUELOVE'S STORY

Ada Truelove's father, Herbert, was a man to be proud of. On 18 December 1897, when he was twenty-five years old, he had walked to Huddersfield Registry Office to marry housemaid Jane Aspinall. For the ceremony Herbert wore a black coat which a clergyman had given him in return for doing some labouring work. A couple of witnesses were brought in from the street; on the wedding certificate their names appeared as Oscar R. Davies and Ralph Oddy. Herbert thanked them and gave them threepence for their trouble.

As the newly weds emerged from the registry office a fellow with a box organ was playing a mournful tune, 'Just another fatal wedding, just another broken heart . . .'; at that moment a chill struck Jane's heart, as though in presentiment of tragedies that lay in store.

They hadn't to wait long. As they trudged back home, with just enough money between them to buy a quarter stone of flour for Jane to begin baking bread there and then, they saw a fire at Fartown Green. Without a thought, Herbert rushed into the stable to try and save a horse – the coat was burned right off his back. He'd kept his cap on, though, he didn't want his hair burning.

What a wedding day! But also what a wonderful indication of the selfless nature of the man Jane had married – rushing regardless into the stable's flames to rescue a terrified animal. Herbert was to suffer from epilepsy later in life; one wonders if traumas bring on illnesses. . . .

The couple rented a house on Bracken Hall Road for a

shilling a week. A woman lived next door with a 'tally' man and both were constantly getting drunk. The pair had a small child, Freddy. One day when Freddy was crying, Jane offered to look after him. In a drunken rage the woman picked up a zinc bucket and hurled it at the new wife. Jane's head bled profusely, but there was no money to pay for a doctor, so she had to minister to it as best she could. She bore the scar until her dying day.

To offset the grinding poverty, all around their home was beautiful, unspoiled countryside. Nearby was Newhouse Wood, where grew celandines, wood anemones, periwinkles, wood sorrel and 'stinking' onions. And it was a toss up which bird sang the loveliest song, the nightingale or the skylark. How Jane and Herbert listened for the first cuckoo, its note heralding the spring.

In the early days of their marriage Herbert was employed as a coal trammer. Neither he nor Jane could write, so each had made a cross on their wedding certificate. Later, he taught himself to read, buying an ABC book for a penny in the market. He wanted to be able to read the Bible.

Herbert's father had been a shoemaker, and had taught Herbert how to make sandals out of old felt hats, cutting a sole out and holding it together with a piece of string. Jane took washing in to help eke out their meagre finances. They were grateful for small mercies – such as the umbrella given to her by a missionary.

Herbert had never known what it was to have plenty of money. His mother had died when he was young, and after that his father had gone into a kind of decline. Though his own family had no shoes, he continued to make them for others, and to teach at Sunday school. Sometimes there was no food at all, and the little boy, Herbert, went to see if his 'aunt Saraellen' (Sarah Ellen) had any to spare. There was a ham bone in a cupboard going green with mould, but the child was so hungry he gnawed away at it. Even so, a doctor at that time maintained, 'I'd rather treat a person who's been clammed to death than an obese one.' How many times had he gone hungry?

There are pleasures in the poorest of lives if they are looked for. As a child Herbert adored drawing on the pavement with a sharp pointed stone, – he had no toys, but that was enough to make him happy.

Though an animal lover, Herbert shot a pheasant if he saw one rather than see his wife go hungry. Since everyone was in the same boat, most neighbours helped each other whenever they could, using what talents they had to assist those in need. Susannah Hartley, who lived in a yard called Duke Fold, at Sheepridge, laid people out when they died. Not surprisingly, her favourite song was rather macabre:

> If you knew the baby's fingers
> Clasped against the window pane
> Would be stiff and cold tomorrow,
> Never trouble us again,
> Would the bright eyes of your darling,
> Catch the frown upon your brow?
> Would the print of baby's fingers,
> Vex us then as they do now?

Jane and Herbert named their first child Harold. He had a skin so delicate and fair it was almost transparent. Sadly, he didn't live long. But then John arrived, followed by Edith, then Ada.

His family completed, Herbert eked out a living as a handyman on local farms, and selling the occasional painting. Although he never had a drawing lesson in his life, he was pronounced a genius by all who saw his drawings and paintings. One gentleman was so impressed he even offered him the opportunity to go to college in London, but Herbert refused. The shallow city life was not for him. Nor was he interested in fame. For him there were more important things in life. He always had a deep respect for 'The Word of God', saying, 'A man ceases to live in the true sense if he ceases to wonder and marvel at the handiwork of God.'

So true to life were his paintings that one, depicting a sheepdog called Kruger, was painted with a small patch of white hair on his chest. However, when presented with the painting, 'Kru's' owners remarked that their dog had no white patch. Truelove, who had only studied the dog for a minute or two before going home and setting to with his brushes, asserted confidently, 'If I have painted him with a white patch, he has a white patch.' Kruger was summoned, and, sure enough, there was the marking which had hitherto gone unobserved by his owners.

Eccentrics roamed those Pennine villages. When the Trueloves lived in a cottage near Fell Greave Farm, Emma Hinchliffe added their name to her list of thirty 'calling spots'. Emma always wore a sturdy apron with huge pockets, where were transported hammer, nails, rolls of bandages, smelling salts (in case people were 'taken bad'), finger plasters and other odds and ends that might come in handy on her travels. She looked upon her unorthodox assistance as her ministry in life – and received free dinners at all the places she visited.

She would turn up at the Trueloves every thirty days, wearing her habitual old felt hat that looked rather like a Spanish sombrero. That hat eventually turned green with age. If a gate had broken down, Emma's hand dived into her walking hardware shop of a pinafore and set to work. She sang in the chapel choir, but even in the choir stalls the apron and its contents were in place. Emma could also bark like a dog to entertain her clients.

Herbert hadn't any curtains at the windows of his home and became fed up with a neighbour, Mrs Hart, a 'know-all' who would peer in to see what they were doing, so he placed pots of geraniums along the windowsill to serve as a screen. Unfortunately, although his 'screen' had its own charm, it did nothing to shut out the strident voice:

'Have yer getten up yet, Janey?'

The couple acquired a broken down phonograph from somewhere; it was a parlour model with cylinders like huge cannons and a great big horn. Indistinctly, but miraculously, could be heard 'Nearer My God to Thee', 'The Sinking of the Titanic', even the great Dame Clara Butt booming out in that deep contralto voice, 'Abide with Me'. On a lighter note they could listen to 'Tis the Last Rose of Summer' and 'My Wild Irish Rose'. What wonders there were in the world! A little boy who used to call to see them never failed to demand, 'Put a toon on, Ada.'

Mrs Hart didn't take the hint, seeing the tall geranium screen, so after a while Herbert erected a fence, to 'retard her progress'.

Though poor in material terms, they were enriched by a

never-ending stock of stories of days gone by that enthralled Ada. There was the time a friend of Herbert's mother was mixing dough, her husband snoring in his rocking chair, when a sudden rush of soot swooshed down the chimney – and all over the dough rising before the fire. The bakeress was utterly distraught. What a catastrophe!

'Never mind, lass. Mix it up and make it into currant bread' advised her husband, solving the problem. They couldn't afford to waste it.

When Ada's brother John was old enough he joined the Boy Scouts, and adhered rigorously to the Scout motto 'Be prepared'. He worked for Cliffords, the cardboard tube makers, at Fartown. Ada worshipped her big brother John. One winter Thursday, after returning home from the heat of his workplace, Ada asked if she could spread treacle on his bread for his tea.

The simple repast finished, he donned his Scout hat, shorts and pennant, kissed Ada, then set off to walk to Northgate in town. It was freezing cold and when John reached Northgate he was waylaid by a tramp who asked, 'Will you help me, lad? I want a workhouse but I don't know the way . . .' The kind-hearted Boy Scout didn't simply give him directions how to walk to Crosland Moor Workhouse but accompanied the old man right to the door. Then walked all the way back into town, then home to Sheepridge.

Probably as a result of working all day in overpowering heat, then being out in the bitterly cold night air doing that good turn, the seventeen-year-old John began hallucinating during the early hours, and succumbed to pneumonia. Herbert walked as fast as he could to get a doctor, but it was too late. The Trueloves' second son had passed away.

Ada was so proud to have been allowed to spread treacle on his bread the day before, for such a marvellous person as John. She kept his Scout's pennant as a treasured memento. Often she recalled the Christmas when her brother had been given an old Meccano set by a neighbour. How clever, how magnificent were the edifices John used to make – he'd never allow 'our Edith' within a mile of his prized possession. But John's favourite sister Ada was always allowed to stand and watch.

Lack of material goods was amply made up for by imagination, and the free bounty of the countryside. Ada and Edith used to pretend to be Red Indians, wearing hens' feathers in their hair, faces daubed a wild-looking purple with elderberry juice.

Food was not plentiful. At Woodhouse School the children were given breakfast on weekday mornings by caretakers Mr and Mrs Baxendale – a slice of bread each, thinly spread with a cheap plum jam, and cocoa without milk. But doubtless, after walking all the way from Bradley Bar – they had since gone to live at the Old Toll House, 337 Bradley Road – that cocoa tasted like nectar to an empty stomach. Indeed, Ada vows she never tasted any as good.

Mid-day dinner at school consisted of an Oxo cube, carried in their pockets, placed in a mug into which boiling water was poured to make a 'nourishing' drink, and another slice of bread.

'What we ate when we went home for tea was nobody's business. . . .'

Only four when she began school, Ada wore a garment cut down from a grown-up's discarded coat. The coarse material was simply sewn up the front. 'Mother was no seamstress,' smiled Ada affectionately. She recalled how the teacher ordered, 'Take your coat off, Truelove.'

'I can't,' replied the awestruck infant.

'Why?' demanded Miss Whoever-it-was.

'There's nothing underneath,' explained the child.

Edith and Ada never once thought to hang up a stocking on Christmas Eve, yet neither was ever bitter about the lack of presents. There were potatoes and turnips in the garden, and a huge holly tree up Fixby Road in the wood, from where their father could haul home branches laden down with big, deep crimson berries to adorn their home. The children rejoiced with him at the munificence of the woods, especially when farmer Kershaw suggested, 'Now, Truelove, get me a couple of hares.' After Herbert had duly caught them, the farmer said, 'Merry Christmas – and take one home for yourself.'

Among their country pursuits Ada and Edith used to knit 'purse nets' to snare rabbits, and Herbert was often called upon to clear rats from barns.

One winter, in the days when winters really *were* winters, Brier Hill, a neighbouring farmhouse, was snowbound for weeks, and the coalman, Mr Griffiths, was unable to get through the drifts with his lorry to deliver the much-needed fuel. Herbert was always ready to help anyone in trouble. Now he was particularly anxious as there were small children in the farmhouse who would be terribly cold. He advised the coalman to leave the coal with him – somehow he'd see that it was delivered.

Ada and Edith watched in trepidation as the gaunt figure of their father, habitual red scarf knotted round his neck, set off, bowed low beneath a sackful of coal. They helped him over a wall only to gasp with dismay as he sank from view beneath the drifts. But up he came and ploughed a pathway through. The return journey, with sacks empty, was much easier.

Often it's those with the kindest hearts who seem to fare badly. Another of his jobs was to wheel out an elderly, well-off lady in her old-fashioned bath chair with a wheel at the front. One day the wheel suddenly came in contact with a brick – Herbert didn't notice until it was too late and the old lady was catapulted into a bed of nettles. Herbert was sacked, making the little family (Jane had died by that time) even worse off than before.

In spite of such setbacks Herbert always wanted to do the best he could for his daughters. Christmas was Christmas, and he determined to give them a present each. Earlier, the old lady, his former employer, had given him a cast-off ancient fur coat, bare in patches, to 'see if he could do something with it'. Herbert cut out the best bits, which even so still left pathetically mangy areas, fashioning them into a bear. He stuffed it with old rags, stitched it together, and fixed in a couple of black boot buttons for eyes. For Edith, he had managed to get a little book, *Dollie Pie*.

The children slept beneath what had once been an Alhambra quilt, but had now become so patched that hardly any of the original design could be discerned. To compensate, heated firebricks wrapped in bits of old cloth were placed in the bed to warm it up a bit, and overcoats thrown over for extra weight and warmth.

When they were asleep, Herbert crept upstairs and suspended the 'bear' by a piece of cord from the bed rail. Awakened by the sound of a brass band and carol singing, Ada's unsuspecting gaze fell on the 'monstrosity' slung over her bed.

'I couldn't have been more stunned if I'd observed Sherpa Tensing coming up the Himalayas,' she laughed. However, she realized that it was meant to be a teddy bear, lovingly made, so carted it round with her for a long time afterwards. It had, after all, been meant to please her, and the youngsters were thankful for whatever came their way.

Despite poverty, they were happy and contented. Jesus the Saviour was born, there were sticks a plenty to light the fire, their father had even managed to buy some penny strips of green and pink crêpe paper from the Top Market for them to make decorations. They curled the papers with a blunt knife, and then wound them round wire. The Toll House cottage was quite transformed when they had finished! A permanent feature of the home was a gipsy caravan Herbert had made, with miniature figures and a blazing fire created from crinkled shiny red paper. It was admired by all who saw it.

Ada was never bitter about the shortcomings of her childhood with its lack of material possessions. Her life then was overflowing with what really matters – kind hearts, the beauty of the countryside in its different seasons, and, perhaps best of all, a talented artist for a father, who could draw and paint pictures so true to life that Ada almost expected the birds and animals to move. Christmas was where it should be, in the heart, not in the shops. And her Christmas bear was remembered with the utmost affection ever afterwards.

Summertime was delightful. In the rambling cottage garden grew rhubarb galore, raspberries, strawberries and vegetables. Herbert often sat in the broken-down summer house at the bottom of the long garden, keeping a watchful eye out for any intruders intent on raiding the goods. Farmers' dogs were sometimes 'boarded' with him while Herbert trained them to retrieve. He also broke in horses. Anything to do with birds, animals, or the countryside, and Herbert Truelove was your man.

He kept ferrets in hutches. Once one of them nipped his finger to the bone when he reached for it and Herbert was forced to throttle it before the ferret released its hold. Not taking any chances, Ada wore gloves on the occasions she had to deal with them. Even Herbert's faithful dog, Gipsy, was a bit wary of those ferrets. Not so of rats. These often found their way into

Herbert Truelove and his dog Gipsy

haystacks when Gipsy would shake them so violently they expired – gladly.

After dining on a rabbit, a ferret curled up and slept the meal off for a couple of days. Sometimes Herbert caught sparrows in a trap to feed them with. This entailed the use of a fine net frame which was perched precariously so that when Herbert pulled a string the net dropped, trapping the victim. The bird's neck was then twisted and it was 'chucked into the ferret'. And there was one unpleasant period when the ends of their paws dropped off due to foot rot.

Herbert was famed locally for his country lore. He was expert at removing moles, which most people found impossible to deal with, and they willingly paid him to do the job for them. As a boy, he preferred bird nesting, spending days in the open air, to school.

It was a rough existence, but no day was ever the same. In what leisure time he had Herbert became a regular reader of

Cage Birds and *Fur and Feather*, besides the daily Bible reading. In the evening he read by the light of an oil lamp at the window of the Toll House. His children's first beds were a couple of orange boxes, extended with more boxes as they grew. Edith having been born on a Christmas Day, her mother had had a present of a new baby, if nothing else.

Among the other well-known figures in the area was Miss Marjorie Brook, who lived at the Warrenfield, a big house on Sheepridge Road. She used to ride to hounds side-saddle. Then there was what used to be termed – not in any cruel manner – the village idiot. His mother made him wear an apron over his trousers, to deter him from showing all and sundry what was inside them. One day a Miss Ford was on her rounds giving out church magazines (it was whispered she had designs on the vicar) when the lad caught sight of her. Thinking her a likely kind of person to display his wares to, he chased her all over the village. Perhaps the poor lad's infirmity was in no way surprising – the lad's father was his mother's brother.

One fellow trundled pie and peas round, always wearing a flower in his lapel and sporting a wing collar. Ada recalls the pie crust having 'a bit of a funny taste – like sump oil' while the pie seller's neck was permanently tilted to one side, in questioning attitude.

Dustbinmen occasionally came across discarded 'Come to Jesus' winged collars, and put them on during working hours for a laugh. Then there was Gipsy Smith who lived in Post Office Yard, Castlegate, near the town centre, and 'Gipsy Bob' who never had any clothes that fitted him, and looked, according to Ada, 'kind of a toe rag'. He walked with the aid of a crutch – and wasn't averse to using it in a dispute, either.

Before the widening of the road in the early thirties, Bradley Lane was a pretty country pathway. Herbert Truelove, together with his daughters Edith and Ada, dwelt in almost splendid isolation when they first went to live at the Toll House. Jane had died, Herbert had developed epilepsy. Even when she was no more than a child, Ada knew instinctively what to do when her father fell down in a fit. They also knew never to go near the cellar head as there was a well down there, its depths unimaginable to the girls.

Richard Spedding had lived in the house before them, and it was in that same long cottage garden that his wife had accidentally poked a raspberry cane into her eye and been blinded as the wind blew the canes to and fro. Spedding had been a ship's doctor in 1911, and sported a waxed moustache, so stiff at the ends that it seemed the moustache itself was capable of blinding anyone who ventured too near!

Later, Herbert acquired a donkey, Jenny, who could be seen trundling a load of rhubarb and other seasonable vegetables for sale. One morning Jenny decided she wasn't going to walk a step further; on another day she was in entirely different mood. When Herbert emerged from a cottage where he'd been selling a bundle of rhubarb, Jenny was charging along to Brighouse – the donkey had bolted with the rest of his wares.

If the children wanted a drink of water from a cattle trough nearby they waited, heeding their dead mother's warnings, until the horses and cattle had all gone and the water was running clear again.

When Ada was fifteen, gipsies encamped nearby. One of them was about to give birth beneath a hedge so another made a fire in the field, piling sticks on top of one another. Herbert thought his daughter 'a bit young to be involved in that sort of thing' when one of the gipsies asked Ada to carry out buckets of water to them. But under the circumstances, he gave his consent, in spite of his misgivings.

Travellers and hikers always made a beeline for the Trueloves' homestead. Ada recalled how, in the early 1920s, a party of vegetarians knocked at the door one Saturday. For a moment Herbert was nonplussed when they requested a drink of tea, but then he hospitably 'mashed' enough for all fifteen. The party had to take their refreshment standing up, drinking the welcome brew unceremoniously, out of jam-jars – there weren't enough chairs for guests.

But how the company enjoyed themselves! A collection was taken, and 10 shillings handed over, which was a marvellous windfall for the little family. The vegetarians even asked if they could call again. It had all been 'a bit of a pantomime' according to Ada – whopping big iron kettle on the fire, a similar sized jug, and Ada pouring tea into the lined up jam-jars. Afterwards they washed up with water from the other kettle, which had red rust inside. Such 'smash and grab raids', where good humour and hospitality abound, were appreciated as far superior to the most lavish repast with ill-tempered hosts. All the while Jenny brayed in her brick stable at the bottom of the garden, the scent of mixed flowers sweetly heavy in the summer air.

Jenny, as well as Herbert, was becoming a well-known character in her own right. There was the comic occasion when she and Herbert were approaching Brighouse and Jenny came to an abrupt standstill. Bus drivers jumped out, Herbert tried to push the donkey – everything came to a standstill. What a procession!

A bit of luck came their way, however, when a lady in Mirfield let them have a sewing machine for 10 shillings. There was an ornamental box to put over the machine when it was not in use. Obliging for once, Jenny pulled the machine home on the cart.

Itching to make the most of their new possession, Edith and Ada set themselves up as dress designers. They had no patterns, and the first garments they engineered for themselves made them feel as though they were walking around in straightjackets – 'a right mullock'. The dresses were fashioned out of old sheets. They also had a go at making a pair of knickers each. But when Ada started walking, hers split right down the middle.

During this period trade was brisk for Herbert. Joe Butterworth brought ponies for him to break in. One, a grey roan, had been shell-shocked in the Great War. She was a beauty but, hardly surprising, her experiences had made her behaviour unpredictable. One day Herbert, Joe and 'hoss' had paused for a cheese sandwich on their travels, tying the horse to a sign post while they went inside a hostelry. Suddenly, they heard a wild shriek. They dashed outside to see the horse, with the cart still harnessed to it, splayed out on all four legs. Truelove and the horse ended up on all fours, the shafts of the cart up in the air. Ada thought the horse looked as if it were doing the rhumba. She, of course, wasn't allowed by her father to enter public houses, and so had seen the entire performance from start to finish. Somehow or other Joe, Herbert and the landlord managed to extricate themselves from the entanglement and life resumed an orderly course.

Ada loved the wild roses blooming in the hedgerows, and the dog roses which children referred to as 'Moon Pennies'. Gipsies boiled nettles to rinse their hair, keeping it shiny and glossy.

Motor waggons from Wales came to Yorkshire in the 1926 Depression, decrepit old vehicles sent to fetch coal which was in short supply down there. Herbert helped them dig coal out of a day hole. If the engine of a waggon overheated, they took water from a well down Bradley Lane to cool it.

Edith was becoming full of romantic ideas as she left childhood behind. A friend passed on her copies of *Home Chat* and *Home Notes*, dog-eared and tatty by the time Edith laid eager hands on the weekly magazines, but prized nevertheless as they were full of hints on how to beautify oneself, and make young men fall head over heels in love. There were also romantic stories and serials, making Edith wish the days away until the next instalment. So eager was she to meet the opposite sex that she even asked Mrs Hudson if her son Walter was married!

Round about that time Edith and her friend Hannah Humpleby attended Battyford chapel. Mr Edwards gave an invitation to those who wanted to serve the Lord, the result of which was that both Edith and Ada joined the Salvation Army.

Their circle of friends enlarged, and Mrs Haygarth, whose husband worked for Kershaw's Farm as a labourer, invited the sisters to tea. Mrs Haygarth had a vivid imagination. What stories she told Ada and Edith in that Bradley Farm Cottage one teatime in 1930!

Their hostess was larger than life in every way, wearing a Salvation Army dress she had bought with a 'Follow Me Lad' kind of nurse's train hanging down her back. Ada recalls that she had baked some mint pasty for their tea which proved to be 'hard as rubber bullets'.

Numerous cats wandered in and out of Mrs Haygarth's cottage. One, Mrs Haygarth assured her guests, was a performing cat. Edith was mesmerized as the lady told them that when she uttered three magic words, the cat would perform.

Elsie, as their hostess invited the girls to call her, picked up a bread knife. Striking the recumbent cat with a sharp tap from the shaft of the knife, she commanded imperiously, 'Piss, puss, piss'. Sure enough, up the performing cat leapt. 'You see, it obeys my voice,' said Mrs Haygarth. Edith nearly exploded in utter amazement, never having heard such words in her life before nor seen such a reaction. Then the cat turned round and licked its assaulted back end.

While his wife entertained her guests Mr Haygarth was slaving away as usual on the farm, 'mucking beasts out'. His only leisure time was walking from Bradley Bar into Huddersfield on Saturday evenings to listen to the Salvation Army Band playing in the Market Square. Then he walked back.

Edith and Ada went to work in Walter Berry's mill when they left school. A friend who worked with them asked Ada to be one of her bridesmaids when she married, but only on condition that Ada had one of the fancy new 'perms'. Ada wasn't at all keen about being under one of those big 'drier machines' – besides, she had smelt other girls' hair after they'd subjected themselves to 'lotions and stuff', and it was terrible. Just like peardrops in a heat wave. However, always one to oblige, she took the plunge, taking the precaution of prudently putting a pair of scissors into her handbag so she could cut her hair off at the ends if a fire started while she was under one of those things!

Ada Truelove, when working at Walter Berry's mill

All that palaver, and on the big day itself, the bride had such big feet, she hadn't managed to find a pair of white shoes to fit. Nevertheless, something white had to be worn so she waddled up the aisle, a pair of her father's white cricket boots just visible underneath her wedding dress.

Ada's first wage was 15s. 2d. At Christmas, every employee was presented with a goose. There were some heated exchanges provoked by this gesture among those who only had one family member working at the mill as even if three or more from a single family were employed, each was given a goose regardless. So Edith and Ada received a goose each. Edith was terrified of handling dead birds, so Ada slung both over her shoulders for the long trek home to the Toll House. Once there, the geese were laid to rest on a stone in the pantry. Next day one was sold to a neighbour for 5 shillings. He was an eccentric man who, earlier that year, had transported his belongings to his new abode inside a coffin on a horse and cart. Thereafter he kept his blankets in the coffin.

At the mill, lavatories were in a long line, with no locks. Nor was it unknown for a boss to kick a door in if a girl had been absent from her work for longer than he thought she needed. 'Come on, lass, let's have thi out o' theer,' he'd grumble. Hardly more comfortable, there was a small room where employees could eat their mid-day meal either standing or sitting on old skips. Conditions were hard. In those days workers were threatened with the sack – dismissal – for the slightest misdemeanour.

Ada wore black Linzi aprons and dust caps to work, bought from Berry's stall in the Top Market. Despite non-stop sheer 'graft' at work and home mill girls went about smiling, whistling and singing, copying Gracie Fields belting out 'Sally' and 'The Biggest Aspidistra in the World'. Hymns were more to Ada's taste, though. Occasionally she took her Salvation Army tambourine to the mill and encouraged the other workers to sing, 'Come and Join Us, Come and Join Us, Come and join our Happy Throng.'

Reminiscing over her time as a mill girl, Ada recalled how one of her colleagues, Joyce Lindley, was convinced that another girl had something wrong with her. 'She broke wind umpteen times a day.' The poor girl was also afflicted in another way. For some reason she only had a 'few sprigs' of hair, so she regularly applied

Edward's Harlene Hair Tonic, rubbing it into her scalp at break time in an effort to produce glorious, luxuriant hair like the girl pictured on the bottle.

Not having much success, the winder bought a wig. Even then, fate was against her. At home-time one afternoon a gale blew up as workers came out from the mill. A hat was pinned to the wig – both flew off onto the tramlines. Ada, always one to look on the bright side, remarked how fortunate the poor girl was. Had the hat pin not been pinned to the wig, it could have pierced her brain!

When the annual Wakes Week arrived and the mill closed down for the holiday – no pay for employees then – Ada spent the week washing old overcoats, used as blankets from the beds, and helping her father, taking out market garden goods with Jenny the donkey. Edith, who married in 1932, was more concerned with the contents of *Home Chat* and *Home Notes*.

Edith met her husband Fred as a result of her friendship with his sister, Doris. The parentless brother and sister lived in an orphanage down Fitzwilliam Street in Huddersfield, before finding lodgings with a Madam Purvis. Fred, who was fond of gardening, had a saying, 'It's all done wi't bend o't back.' It was his stock reply to most queries and problems, gardening or otherwise.

Edith had been aided and abetted in her thirst for fashion by Hilda, the grocer's wife. The young Misses Truelove called at their village shop every Friday on their way home from the mill,

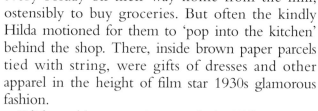

ostensibly to buy groceries. But often the kindly Hilda motioned for them to 'pop into the kitchen' behind the shop. There, inside brown paper parcels tied with string, were gifts of dresses and other apparel in the height of film star 1930s glamorous fashion.

Edith could never wait to reach the Toll House to have a peep. Halfway up the country lane curiosity would overcome her, parcels were stood on the dry stone wall, and joy filled her being as she spied pretty satins, crêpes de Chine and smart, up-to-the-minute costumes and, occasionally, a coat and hat.

The bride-to-be had read in the magazines that a bride should have 'something borrowed,

Ada Truelove in 1939

something blue' on her wedding morn, so the grocer's wife offered to lend Edith her own wedding veil. Edith couldn't afford to have it dry cleaned, but since it had last been worn in 1923, it could do with freshening up. Foregoing the luxury of the dry cleaners, Ada carefully washed it in Lux flakes instead, and it 'came up beautifully'.

Ada had been to see the landlady of the house where Edith's husband-to-be lodged, and ascertained that the young man was an honest, God-fearing person and so quite suitable as a match for Edith. Meanwhile Edith, stars in her eyes, often talked about the way Mrs Taylor, the grocer's wife, rolled her eyes as a signal for them to enter 'The Hall of Fashion' – the back kitchen – after appearing in the shop doorway 'like an angel from the realms of splendour – all dolled up with plenty of ruddle [rouge] while moving around in an exotic aura of either Evening in Paris, Ashes of Roses, Devon Violets, or Phul-Nana perfume'.

That Wakes Week in 1932, Ada white-washed the ceiling in preparation for the happy event and Herbert tramped down to the grocer's to buy unsold bread and teacakes left over from Saturday – 'seemingly more interested in his lifestock than any wedding', laughed Ada. Eggs at the Toll House were to sell, not to be used for baking or their own consumption, except for the occasional treat.

Another day Herbert managed a Herculean task. He had promised to make a hen hut for Mr Taylor, and deliver it. He carried it on his back all the way down the old lane, up a field, then deposited it in the grocer's henyard. Ever mindful of his wellbeing, Ada accompanied him in case he suffered an epileptic fit on the way. To keep his spirits up he sang 'Should auld acquaintance be forgot' as he staggered along. A man of his word, yet as he thankfully heaved the hut off his back he declared, 'It's the first and last time I'll ever carry a hen hut on me back.'

Edith bought a magnificent wedding dress from Price's Gown Emporium, with leg-o'-mutton sleeves that almost reached the width of the aisle; she would look the epitome of a perfect *Home Chat* bride. It was Wakes Week and what joy, what bliss, as she and her Fred married in Queen Street Mission.

Bridesmaid Doris, Fred's sister, wore a floral voile gown and large floppy picture hat. Ada would have felt out of place wearing her Salvation Army uniform, so only wore the bonnet, with a navy blue mid-calf length dress which cost £35, an extraordinarily extravagant purchase prompted purely by sisterly love. The dress lasted a lifetime.

Then, with Edith married and gone to live happily ever after with Fred, Ada returned to the Toll Bar house to look after her father. Poor Edith's happiness was later jeopardized when, never having enjoyed good eyesight, her left eye had to be removed and a glass one put in. At first, Edith daren't attend to the afflicted area herself so kind-hearted Ada, who luckily had a stronger stomach, had to wash out the back of the eye for her. One day a neighbour bustled in, interrupting the proceedings.

'Nah then, Edith, now you've had a new eye put in, can yer see any better with it?'

Ada never could resist a plea for assistance, despite never knowing material wealth herself. One Friday, walking up the road from the mill, she came upon Lucy Jowett, a maiden lady who went out cleaning to 'keep body and soul together'. She was a gentle, timid little person who adored all animals. Stray cats gravitated to her home. Lucy even begged the grocer for any stale bits of cheese that 'might be going off a bit' so she could put some on the hearth for a 'sweet little mouse' that somehow eluded the attentions of the numerous 'pussies' that had attached themselves to Lucy in her little terrace house.

That particular evening Ada was just approaching Lucy's as the little elderly lady was slowly walking down her garden path, handkerchief clutched to her eyes, sobbing in a truly heart-rending manner. Between sobs she told the sympathetic Ada how she had arrived at her work a little late that morning and, as a result, the man who employed her had refused to pay her half crown wages. Without hesitation or further thought, knowing how much it would cost to buy milk for all the twenty or so cats, Ada pressed her own wage into Lucy's hand with a warm, 'God bless you, Lucy.' Her generosity brought tears of amazed gratitude into the other lady's eyes. For Ada that was reward enough. She had been used to making do with little all her life, it wouldn't hurt her to do it again. And how could she be happy, knowing someone else was suffering? As the saying used to go, 'Never a day without a deed to crown it.'

Herbert owned a Winchester repeater rifle which was propped

up in one corner at the Toll Bar house. He had three guns altogether and was a marvellous shot, always aiming for the head. Whatever else befell father and daughter, they wouldn't starve. What with the vegetables in the garden, the stale teacakes from Taylors – ostensibly for the hens – and sticks from the woods to light the fire. Their needs were simple, and they trusted in the Lord.

Local preachers such as Ada not uncommonly came up against hazards when invited to a parishioner's for mid-day dinner on a Sunday. After preaching at Wiggan Lane, Sheepridge, one Sunday morning Ada was provided with hospitality at a house in Sunny View, a row of stone terrace houses. When she went in, a 'great whopping iron pan was on the fire, potatoes and turnip in that, a cow heel simmering in another'. The whole place was in such an uproar one would have thought the occupants were 'flitting' (removing). On the table, the patterned oilcloth that served as a cloth was all stuck up with grease. Not very inviting.

Mrs Sykes, who was doling out the meal, weighed twenty-two stones. She had been to a prize-giving a week or two previously for regular attendance and was furious at only being awarded second prize. She re-enacted the tale to Ada while shaking the pans to loosen the burnt bits.

'I told 'em I'd been every Sunday. "Calm yourself, Mrs Sykes," the vicar droned, but ah retorted, "Calm be buggared!"'

After the cow heel course some sort of trifle was sloshed on to their saucers. Then Ada said Grace, thanking the Lord for what they had received.

When money was scarce, Herbert dried rhubarb leaves and made them into a kind of tobacco. No reading matter was allowed on the Sabbath apart from the Bible. *Home Chat* and *Home Notes* were definitely taboo. No washing was ever done or hung out on that day – it would have been unthinkable. And if any item had been forgotten at the shop, then they just had to wait until it opened again on Monday morning.

Ada called Mrs Hudson, who was employed at the grocer's to do the rough work, 'Queen of the Blacklead Brushes'. Such was the redness of the cleaner's nose that Ada was sure she must have been born with permanent indigestion. Ada was never bothered about fashion as her sister Edith was; she was always quite content with the 'rejects of the rejects'.

However, inspired by some of the household tips in *Home Chat* or *Home Notes*, she went to Fowler's in the Top Market one Saturday afternoon and purchased a bottle of black enamel. Full of enthusiasm, she returned to the Toll House and applied it to the Yorkshire range. But somehow it all went wrong and came up in bubbles, and there was almost as much black on Ada's face as on the range. When her father came in he exclaimed in amazement, 'What have you been doing, yer crackpot?'

Ada didn't marry until she was fifty-seven. Norman Marston, her husband, lived at Grosvenor Street, Elland. Before the Second World War Norman's aunt, Elizabeth Calvert, a trained teacher, had a private school for six children there. She was a superintendent at the Congregational, so small primary school chairs could be borrowed from the chapel. Elizabeth had married Herbert Malcolm Calvert, a mill owner's son. She was an accomplished poet, Mitre Press publishing her volumes, including such poems as 'Cornfield and Cross', 'Pleasant Paths', 'Quo Vadis – White Banks', 'The Manna Tree', and 'Heart of Daybreak'.

Odd situations followed Ada even in her marriage. Not long after the wedding she went into the cellar to get some treacle which was kept in a big barrel. Unfortunately, she forgot to turn off the tap. When Norman went down into the cellar later, he was greeted with a sticky sight – there was treacle all over the place, like a Mad Hatter's Tea Party. There was treacle 'traipsing over the carpets, up hill and down dale'. Ironically, she now had far more to spare than when, all those years ago, she had so lovingly spread it for her beloved brother John before that fateful night.

Ada and Norman Marston, 19 July 1958

CHAPTER NINE

JOYCE AND JIMMY

'Hard work never killed anybody' is an old maxim adhered to by those who were young in the twenties and thirties. Indeed, it could be that they enjoyed hard work, having been brought up to 'fettling' throughout their childhood in many cases. Even at school, Joyce, and her friend Betty, who lived at the Woolpack pub, looked forward to holidays, not to go away, but to clean and scour the stepping stones in Newhouse Wood.

Armed with buckets, scrubbing brushes and scouring stones, the pair skipped gaily up the old lane to tackle the steps. There was no litter or rubbish in the wood, but if they did find a scrap of paper, it was carefully taken home. They could hardly improve on nature, but the schoolgirls enjoyed the sensation of hard work.

When the steps were scrubbed to their satisfaction, Mrs Pike, whose cottage overlooked the wood, rewarded the industrious pair with apples and pears from her orchard. Sometimes Joyce and Betty picnicked in the woods, taking home-made bread and jam, and either a bottle of pop or simply cupping their hands and 'supping' from the clear, gurgling streams. And what a treat to be allowed to trundle Joyce's wind-up gramophone on a hand cart into the wood, there to listen to bright and breezy tunes! How they enjoyed 'The Man on The Flying Trapeze', 'Red Sails in the Sunset', the sounds of Henry Hall and his Dance Band. 'The Whistler and His Dog' was their favourite, especially the last bit, when the dog barked. Twice.

Law and order ruled the streets in the shape of 'Bobby Ward'. He could be heard whistling and singing as he sat outside on his doorstep assiduously polishing his policeman's boots on warm summer evenings. In those days, a crack on a miscreant's backside from PC Ward or another constable kept those who tended to be a bit unruly firmly under control.

Joyce was amazed when one of the village girls, Mary Wolfenden, and her family acquired a 'posh' bath which they installed in a downstairs room. Before use its wooden lid had to be lifted, so when it covered the window Ada knew someone was having a bath. Most folk made do with tin baths, brought up from the cellar on Friday, bath night, and laboriously filled with hot water from the Yorkshire range.

Schoolchildren of the 1930s knew that if they did anything wrong teachers would punish them. Joyce and Betty joined the Girl Guides and meetings were held in the council school infants room. Shiny tables were stacked on top of one another when school was over, table legs pointing upwards. On one occasion, before the other guides arrived, Joyce and Betty, adventure uppermost in their minds, took down the topmost polished table, placed it on the wooden floor and took it in turns to sit inside while the other pushed the 'boat' out to sea across the

Joyce Lindley (in the third row back, wearing a beret) at Girl Guides during the 1930s

floor. Next morning, in assembly, Oliver Smith, the headmaster, wanted to know, 'Who is responsible for scratching the top of the infants' class tables?'

Well, being Guides and knowing that sins of omission are as bad as any others, the shamefaced would-be sailors owned up. And were caned first on one hand then the other. They never defaced anything belonging to anyone else again.

As most villagers, the Lindley family weren't weighed down with wealth. One Whitsuntide Mrs Lindley wanted a new costume to wear at the chapel anniversary. She couldn't afford a new one for herself, new outfits for the children being a priority, so she unpicked her old one, washed the pieces, and hung them out on the clothes line to dry. Then she dyed them a different shade before painstakingly stitching them together again. Hey presto! for the time spent, and the cost of a little dye, Mrs Lindley went to chapel smart as anyone.

Every Midsummer Day, about ten in the evening, her neighbour from down the road, Tom Hampshire, always knocked at her door after 'partaking of a few jars', resplendent in dark suit and bowler hat. Sweeping off the bowler in a courteous bow, Tom uttered the same words year after year:

'Good evening, Mrs Lindley, I've come for my piece of spice cake.' She knew to keep back some of her Christmas cake for the Midsummer occasion; it was an annual tradition, and she mustn't be found wanting. As Tom said, 'it's an awfully long time between one Christmas cake and the next.' But if you had a slice halfway through the year the wait was just about bearable. . . .

Joyce, when she began working at Walter Berry's mill, had not to walk as far as Ada and Edith Truelove who had the long country lane to negotiate before even reaching the road. Joyce lived at 1 Hepworth's Buildings, and if it wasn't a foggy or snowy morning could walk it in about ten minutes. Her first job, when she was just fourteen, was as a twister. She remembers that the warehouse was on the ground floor, and then there were three flights of rickety wooden steps leading up to where she worked.

Oliver Strang was her boss. He wore smart shiny black shoes, while the ordinary men's shoes were 'full of muck and grease'. The foreman was Herbert Reed, the manager, Hubert Armitage. Annie Boothroyd perched on a high stool in the mill office.

The hierarchy, of course, never joined in the gossip. One Monday morning the tale went round that Mrs Wolfenden, 'a right acid drop' according to Joyce, had been up to the neck in the Monday washing, steamed up to the eyes over her peggy tub, when the stick had slipped and hit her on the nose. What a shiner!

Relatives often went to tea with the Lindleys. There was Mrs Lindley's brother William Shackleton, who, at the tender age of ten already played the cornet with the Brighouse and Rastrick Band, as well as playing the euphonium at the Crystal Palace in London, where he was awarded a medal. Joyce's great-grandad had been a headmaster, and her Auntie Mabel Hartley was nicknamed 'The Mayoress of Bradley' as she was always fashionably turned out. Grandma Lindley had been in domestic service when young.

In the lovely summer just prior to the outbreak of the Second World War, Joyce and Betty failed to go scrubbing the stepping stones in Newhouse Wood when holiday time came round. Instead they went to Blackpool together. By Monday they had spent all the money they had on clothes. Betty sent a letter to

Grandma Lindley (seated third from right in the front row) who was in domestic service

her father, Reed, at the pub, to send her a 10 shilling note. Lack of money wasn't such a disaster though, not at sixteen. Not a whit put out, they had their photographs taken, smiling happily, with the superintendent of Stanley Park, and knew that something would turn up sooner or later. It usually did.

Joyce Lindley and her friend Betty with the superintendent of Stanley Park, Blackpool

But Joyce's destiny didn't lie in Blackpool; it lay at Castle Hill, near her home town of Huddersfield.

In 1916, at Ashes Common, Castle Hill, District Road Surveyor Joe Mellor married Edith, a domestic servant who had been born in Thurlestone. Edith didn't change her doctor when she married, which entailed a long walk for Joe when his young wife was about to give birth. But though snow was deep on the ground – and up on the top there at Castle Hill it can be deeper than in most Pennine districts – Joe didn't hesitate. He set off across the fields, knee deep in a vast winter wonderland of whiteness, and walked all the way to Penistone where the doctor lived.

That Sunday morning the doctor rode on horseback to attend to Edith, while Joe, his mission accomplished, returned home on foot, arriving not long after the doctor. Had something gone wrong that day, Jimmy Mellor would not have lived to meet and marry Joyce Lindley in future years.

But Joe walked everywhere, and enjoyed it. The doctor pronounced that he had 'a heart like a beast', it was so strong. He and his wife lived in one of the pair of cottages built by Samuel Joseph Mellor, as indicated on a plaque at the front of the property. Samuel's son James became a farmer, then worked for the local Board of Works as District Road Surveyor. He died in 1914. Joe, one of James's four sons, born in 1879, started work at thirteen, stone napping, mashing tea in stone jars, later turning to dry stone walling and masonry work. It was when he progressed to become Huddersfield Corporation Road Surveyor, under the Borough Engineer's Department, that his work provided continual exercise, for he had to walk miles every day throughout his area.

During severe snowfalls he shovelled paths out from the cottages in the early morning, then down Kaye Lane to his depot and yard at the top of Westgate, Aldmondbury. On two occasions his family saw him on the Friday night then not again until mid-day Sunday, at dinnertime. There was no overtime pay, but Joe worked regardless, a dedicated man whose main priority was keeping the job going.

Sometimes, Irish labourers turned up from the Labour Exchange. If any had the same name, or was unable to write his name, Joe simply invented one for him, the first that sprang to mind. It was obligatory for every labourer's name to be written in the time keeping and record book. Some of those Irish navvies only had worn-out and lightweight shoes, quite unsuitable for clearing snow and ice from roads and pavements. So kindly Joe lent them old boots he kept in the depot.

On his sixty-fifth birthday, during the Second World War, Mr Jagger, Borough Engineer, congratulated Joe and asked how he had achieved so many years of unbroken service. The reply came, 'I've been lucky, ah reckon, never ailed owt – but I had half a day off to bury my father.' Mr Jagger smiled and patted the loyal workman on the back. 'I think we will overlook that, Joe, and we have had a meeting and would like to re-instate you until you are seventy. Think it over, and let us know tomorrow.'

Joe jumped at the opportunity, and was credited with fifty-seven years' unbroken service, which included service in the First World War in the Royal Engineers. His Corporation Pension was 10 shillings a week, paid each Friday at 2.00 p.m. Joe was seventy-one when he died in 1950.

His son James, known as Jimmy and born that February day in 1920, had a somewhat isolated childhood out there near Castle Hill. But he had a couple of good pals when he became a schoolboy. One summer holiday they decided to climb to the top of Castle Hill Victoria Tower, and play cards on the parapet. They took stones in their pockets to hold the cards down or the swirling wind at that high altitude would have blown them away. They felt themselves to be living out one of the adventure stories in *Boy's Own* or the *Magnet*.

Jimmy Mellor (standing on the left with his cricket bat)

Jimmy and his chum Leonard enjoyed helping out at Wilf Beaumont's farm, especially at haymaking time. Sometimes the boys gathered up manure with their bare hands, put it in wheelbarrows, and sold it to those folk who couldn't be bothered getting it themselves.

One day in the summer holidays they had a terrific idea for a game. Off the couple raced, to the woods near Castle Hill, carrying an empty John West salmon tin each, lids removed. They lined the cans up beneath a tree, which they climbed. 'Then we each had a go to see who could pee into one of them,' grinned Jimmy.

When Jimmy left school he had various jobs. He recalls once being employed by Huddersfield Corporation Repairs Department, but mainly he was a storeman and glass cutter with Jack Abson, 'a first class workman and mate'.

Jimmy married Joyce Lindley – but only after his father proposed to Joyce for him. He was a shy sort of lad! In 1980 he took early retirement after being credited with forty-six years' unbroken service.

In retirement there is plenty of time to relive 'The Good Old Days'. How Jimmy's grandfather had water laid on at Ashes Common, Joe doing all the digging. It cost him 5 shillings. Then there was gas meter reader Nora Dransfield, Jimmy's cousin,

Jimmy and Leonard (holding the cart) at Wilf Beaumont's farm

Joyce Lindley, 10 June 1944

whose round took in the Holmfirth area. She was renowned for frequently enjoying a cuddle with Fenella, the famous Holmfirth tiger. Much more dangerous as far as she was concerned was the day when she had to enter a cellar through a trapdoor. A buxom lady, she became trapped, and could proceed neither up nor down. Despite much pushing and heaving they could not release her so an ambulance had to be sent for.

Joyce's Dad once kicked a chapel door in with his clogs when it refused to open by more orthodox methods. Then there was a never-to-be-forgotten Anniversary Sunday at Colnebridge Chapel, when a lady who enjoyed putting on 'airs and graces' turned up beautifully dressed as usual, her outfit topped by a splendid black hat. Unfortunately, she suffered from St Vitus Dance, twitching erratically every so often. So dramatic were her twitches that she overbalanced on the outdoor wooden platform used in fine weather. The unfortunate lady ended up 'sitting in a cowclap' and had to be ushered into the chapel and cleaned up.

On another occasion at chapel one of the ladies had brought her home-baked date pasties. They hadn't cooled off, so they were arranged round an outside drain. When, after the service, the preacher ate one he inadvertently swallowed a stone that had become stuck to his pasty. He couldn't heave it up for what seemed like eternity itself.

Joyce's Dad eked out his wage by taking on an evening newspaper round as well as one on Sunday mornings. For his exertions he earned 8 shillings a week.

Dancing round the maypole in Greenhead Park is another of Joyce's fond memories. It was specially for Sunday school scholars who attended the Band of Hope; in and out they would weave with long colourful ribbons, making the tableau resemble a huge cobweb. 'All mixed up and worked up when practising – but all right on the day.'

Sometimes they were sent to buy shilling lots at Winn's fish shop in town. A mixture of cod, hake, herrings, whatever was left over at closing time. Occasionally a crab was thrown in for good measure. The contents of those parcels lasted all week (one wonders how, they certainly didn't have a fridge). Often there were delicious muffins and oatcakes at teatime.

Joyce recalls how she rather fancied herself as a singer, still having enough energy after a hard day's work in Walter Berry's mill to stand up and sing in Deighton Chapel concerts. Her *pièce de resistance* was 'Because'. 'Because God made Thee Mine, I'll Cherish Thee, Through Life and Darkness Through all time to be . . .'

She progressed to become a mender at Blamires. Workers were 'vetted' before being taken on there. 'You were snooty if you were a mender!' Joyce remembers how they were all referred to as 'snobs' as soon as they were promoted to that high station in life. Her *bête noir* was walking down to work in thick fog, when mill chimneys and coal fires belched out smog, adding to the already misty and moisty November and December mornings as well as being a real health hazard.

'All me "nose holes" used to be full of fog' and black muck streaked my face on arrival at work.' When conditions were icy many mill workers put men's socks over their clogs or shoes so they wouldn't slip.

In the thirties tuppence was the tram fare for a day out at Sunny Vale during the school holidays. Here there was a maze,

Joyce Lindley (standing far left) at Blamires Mill in 1946

helter-skelter, and penny buns and a bottle of pop. Heaven on earth.

As a child Jimmy loved making 'roads' and farms on the floor at home for his toy animals. What an almighty surprise one Christmas morning in the 1920s when good old Santa left a huge present. In the corner of the bedroom stood a roll of lino, tied with string. It unrolled to disclose a boy's delight! Unknown to Jimmy, while he was asleep in the days leading up to Christmas, his Dad had bought the roll of plain linoleum and painted railway lines, road, trees and fields on it. Tunnels were placed there made out of old book spines.

Once Joyce found a skipping rope taken from a grocer's orange box in her Christmas stocking. 'Right hairy stuff, which hurt my legs if it came too near.'

Milkman Albert Beaumont was considered a bit of a tease. One of his favourite tricks was to ask any unsuspecting young girl, 'D' you fancy a drink?' If she innocently said yes, he would lift a cow's teat and squirt milk into her astonished face.

When spending money didn't run to any more sweets, in summer there was always the alternative of 'pinching' a stick of rhubarb and dipping it into a bag of sugar. Hours of pleasure were to be had hunting for 'hairy nuts' in the woods, or digging up garlic in Grimescar Wood when onions were scarce during the Second World War. Then there was the fun to be had breaking icicles off walls in wintertime on the way to school, for 'iced lollies'.

One day when Jimmy was twelve or thereabouts, he saw smoke billowing out of a chimney in Ashes Common. Thinking he could solve the problem, he clambered on to a low roof having first cut a sod of turf. This he dropped over the smoking chimney 'so it hung over nice and comfortable'. Satisfied he had cured the chimney of smoking – a job well done – he was mystified to see the old couple who lived in the cottage emerge a few minutes later, coughing and spluttering. Stew and dumplings had been simmering on their Yorkshire range when a sudden shower of soot cascaded on to that and over them. They thought it must be a flue blockage, and the chimney sweep went round the next day. Wasn't Jimmy relieved when he spied the sweep's brush appear, lifting the sod clear of the chimney. He hadn't slept at all well the night before. . . .

The old couple kept a little shop adjoining the cottage where an ancient coal place door formed the sweet counter. Being a country district, hens roamed freely, often fluttering into the shop and taking a look at the goods as they strutted over the open cardboard boxes.

But such country ways have their drawbacks. Liquorice torpedoes were a popular buy from the shop. One afternoon Jimmy's sister Phyllis bought a pennyworth and handed the white paper cone-shaped bag round. Suddenly she shouted, 'Hey, What's this? It isn't a torpedo—'. Held gingerly between her finger and thumb was a hen dropping. She was made to throw the whole lot on the fire after that.

One of Joyce's school friends and neighbour, Dennis, whose Dad kept a fish and chip shop, enjoyed filling blue sugar bags with manure and stealthily leaving them on the doorstep of an old woman whom the children thought was a witch. Dennis had something of an obsession with manure parcels. Once he made one up, tying it with string, as though a bona fide parcel from the post office, and left it on the local preacher's doorstep. He ran away so quickly he never did find out what happened. 'You're sick upstairs,' school pals insisted, meaning that only someone soft in the head could want to get their fun in such a revolting way. But Dennis thought such pranks better than being bored. And they didn't cost anything.

He had another, equally unsavoury penchant, this time for smearing cow dung along door snecks, making it impossible for the householder to get inside until he'd touched both dung and sneck.

One Easter during the 1930s Dennis and Frank Robinson arranged to go camping. Frank had some blowing cloth that his father had brought home from the mill. The lads also had some broom handles for holding up any tent they might manage to erect, and a kit bag. On Easter Saturday they boarded a tram to Marsden, buying scholar's returns, tuppence each, anticipating a delightful break.

Blakelea, on the moors, was their objective and when they arrived they erected their tent on the upside of a stream, lit a fire, and were soon wolfing down fried bacon and baked beans. It grew dark relatively early, so they were 'in bed' by eight. It 'rained like Hell' during that first night, and they were 'frozen daft'. When dawn broke it was still pelting down. A young married couple on the opposite side of the stream took pity on the boys and made breakfast for them.

In spite of the weather the lads had no intention of becoming downhearted. It was Easter, and they'd gone there to enjoy themselves. They paddled in the stream – it was freezing. And all the time it continued to rain steadily, with no let up throughout the next night either. By the Monday morning they were 'miserable as Hell'. Finally forced to admit defeat, they packed up and made for civilization. Their copies of the *Magnet* and *Funny Wonder* were as soggy as they were.

When they arrived home Dennis's Dad opened his fish and chip shop up, just for them. It smelt like manna from Heaven. 'You're soon back. I thought you were staying till Tuesday,' Fred said. 'Here you are, get these inside yer,' thrusting a big packet of fish and chips into each eager hand. No place like home, indeed.

Edith and Fred Wood, the owners of
the fish and chip shop in Deighton

Joyce had a happier time when she went on a Girl Guides' outing in Bradley Wood. The sun shone and they made delicious apple fritters. One unlucky girl, Beatrice, suffered from insomnia, so only had a cup of hot milk.

When the rag and bone man turned up at the Lindley household one Monday morning, Joyce took it upon herself to rid the house of a bit of what she thought to be old junk so the man would give her a few coppers. As luck would have it, next time her mother wanted to make brisket she went wild – her flat iron couldn't be found anywhere. Full of trepidation, Joyce eventually owned up. 'You idiot – that's what I press my meat with!' she was reprimanded heatedly.

Grandma Lindley used to wear a brown fox fur. Her grandchildren had an exciting time chasing each other with the strong spring clip yelling, 'Adam and Eve and Nip-Me-Well went down to the river to bathe, If Adam and Eve fell in, who was left?' People soon grew wise to the fact never to answer 'Nip-Me-Well'. Old Mrs Lindley was an indulgent grandma and never thought to spoil their fun by telling them to leave her beloved fur alone. But as far as the children were concerned, if you've never been chased round a big kitchen table by someone threatening you with the spring clip of a fox fur, you've never really lived.

CHAPTER TEN

WHEN PATRIOTISM WAS THE ORDER OF THE DAY

Days when patriotism and the cane ruled at Deighton Council School were an integral part of their childhood for Celia Yeo and Dorothy Priestley, later Mrs Smith and Mrs Suthers, respectively.

In the twenties outside school lavatories were the norm – and the tippler variety at Deighton did not give way to flush toilets until the late 1930s. There was only cold running water in the taps, and roller towels for drying, not very hygienic. Occasionally the sinks boasted a scrap of hard green soap. Celia recalls that many a time no water came out of those taps. But, despite all these shortcomings, the school staff managed to instil some dignity and pride into the children. Miss Walker inspected nails and hands for cleanliness, as well as boots and shoes, another teacher played the piano as the pupils marched into school after lining up outside.

On Empire Day, 24 May, a great spirit of patriotism filled the air when the children paraded round the playground waving

Celia Smith, née Yeo (right) and
Dorothy Suthers, née Priestley

their Union Jacks, and singing 'Rule Britannia', 'Land of Hope and Glory', 'Bluebells of Scotland' and 'The Ash Grove', inspirational tunes which lifted childhood spirits above the trivialities of outside toilets and canings for wrong doing. In keeping with the general sentiments, Celia and the others learned Rupert Brooke's patriotic First World War poem by heart: 'If I should die, think only this of me: That there's some corner of a foreign field That is forever England.'

The excitement of Empire Day and other such welcome breaks from classroom routine over, lessons were sometimes enlivened by comical incidents. When new forms of transport were all the rage, one of the teachers, Mr William Goddard, in an innocent attempt to increase the children's general knowledge, got a shock when he asked one of his class, 'What is an aviator?' Quick as a flash, a voice replied, 'Please, Sir, a man who hates the navy!'

When the ICI works was being built at Leeds Road, wooden huts were erected for families of men working on the project and the workers' children attended Deighton School, bringing their dinners wrapped in newspaper. 'Lardy bread', bread smeared with lard and salt, was a perennial favourite. Chests smeared with goose fat, however, were something else, mothers having saved the fat from the Christmas dinner. If you were unlucky enough to sit by a child who had the grease smeared on their chest, the smell in that warm atmosphere could be almost unbearable, especially with children wearing dresses and trousers of thick serge, a material which did not lend itself to frequent washing. In the face of such hazards, playtime came as a welcome relief, with cool, fresh air. Dinnertime was from mid-day to 2.00 p.m. in summer (lessons ended at half past four), and from mid-day to 1.00 p.m. in winter – any longer outside and the children would have been freezing.

There were no school dinners and many children brought sandwiches which they ate in the cloakroom. Some took a 'mashing' of tea and their own pot to a nearby house, where the lady occupant poured boiling water for them to make a hot drink.

At the weekend, children had the excitement of going to Bradley Lane to see how the big new road was progressing.

Charles Henry Yeo,
Celia's father

Celia's father, Charles Henry Yeo, was Chief Superintendent of Highways. The family lived in the old 'bobby hole' (police house) on Leeds Road, opposite the Junction Inn. Mr Yeo was in charge of the 1932 replacement of narrow, winding Bradley Lane by what in those days must have ranked as a super highway.

Celia recalls a more traumatic incident. She had hospital treatment when a child, the memory still vivid of a 'white, net-like object' being placed over her face, despite her frantic struggles to escape. It was chloroform.

Leaving school at fourteen, she went as a 'maid of all work' on a farm where churning the cream into butter was one of her tasks. She was made to turn a large, two-handled churn by herself. Heaving it round became harder and harder as the cream turned to butter. One day the handle suddenly jerked away; Celia was left with a dislodged churn and never forced to work it by herself again.

Another time she was in the fields 'sticking' – gathering blown down branches to use as fuel on the fire, when before her appeared the most beautiful animal she had ever seen, with a huge bushy tail. How she wanted it – so she gave chase. Little did she realize that the fox, for that's what it was, would have torn her to shreds had it been cornered.

The farm was 6 miles from Harrogate, at Kirby Overblow, and a mile from the nearest village. There were no modern facilities whatsoever. 'Plumbing' meant a large water pump in the yard outside the back door with another over a large stone sink in the kitchen. The only lighting on the farm came from oil lamps and candles. Heat came from the huge fire – a whole bucket-full of coal and one of coke were thrown on at every restoking. To one side of it was a large oven, opposite, a huge boiler. Iron bars across the fire held pans so large that at first Celia found it impossible to lift a full one. Those, and the oven, fed a motley array of family and farm labourers. A strange family custom was that of eating massive suet roly-poly pudding with jam oozing out – as a first course.

A large two-handled milk churn

Later, during the Second World War, Celia was in Huddersfield serving as a postwoman. Girls began their shift at the GPO at 6.00 a.m. sharp; if they were so much as two minutes late they were given a black mark. Two black marks resulted in the loss of part of their wages. It was by no means a cushy job.

Coming up to the busy period of Christmas, when casuals swelled the workforce, postwomen started work an hour earlier, at 5 a.m.; the men had to clock in at 4.00 a.m. After the first delivery, it was back to the canteen at the GPO for a new teacake spread with dripping, then to their tables to get second deliveries prepared, and the casuals out on their rounds again, a day's work finishing between five and six o'clock. This harsh routine was somewhat eased by Celia staying at a friend's home in the town centre the last Christmas of the war, so she would manage to be in the office by 5 a.m.

One day she was preparing the mail when all of them heard a strange noise. Accustomed to 'ours' and 'theirs' aeroplanes, they

Postwoman Celia Smith with her van around 1944

instinctively knew that this was something sinister. It passed over, and they learned later that day – Christmas Day – when even so there was one delivery of letters and parcels, that Hitler had sent as a present one of his macabre doodlebugs.

Celia tried to avoid greeting people at Christmas as she pushed their mail through letterboxes not wishing them to think she was touting for a Christmas Box. Casuals put down their mailbags for the last time on Christmas Eve; regulars worked Christmas Day, but did have a day off on Boxing Day.

Celia and her fellow postal workers became adept at finding their way in the blackout during dark winter mornings and evenings as they were only allowed a tiny, dimly shaded torch to see the addresses on letters and doors. However, it taught workers to be careful, precise and accurate. Thanks to early birds like Celia, important mail reached its destination right on time despite the constraints imposed by wartime. Such commitment to duty was an important part of everybody's war effort.

CHAPTER ELEVEN

OH NO, BABIES DON'T COME FROM UNDER GOOSEBERRY BUSHES

Kathleen Bottomley used to believe that babies came out of their mother's side. She had seen a scar on her mother's side, and, not having been told anything different, assumed that a baby emerged from there. She was confirmed in her belief by the fact that there was no baby when she was sent out to play, yet every time neighbour Mrs Boothroyd called to visit her mother a baby was squawking when Kathleen went back in. This happened with a regularity of thirteen months in between each addition to the family.

In the 1920s, one of Kathleen's brothers developed TB. They tried not to have a doctor's bill, but the boy urgently needed attention. Finding the tuppence a week for when the doctor's man called on Friday evenings took some budgeting for. The doctor paid the bill collector to do the undignified job of trying to 'get blood from a stone'. It wasn't that patients didn't want to pay, simply that they didn't have any spare money for more than the most basic necessities of life.

At ten years old, Kathleen did all she could to help, washing the greengrocer's floor for tuppence a time. She gave it to her mother to help pay for the gas. Occasionally the greengrocer also gave the child some apples that weren't fit to sell. As the family never saw fruit at home, they were a Godsend. Mrs Bottomley made big apple pies after scooping the rotten parts out, and Kathleen took one to school to eat at playtime. Money was very tight. Her parents had seven boys and two girls to feed besides

Kathleen. Rent was 6s. 6d. a week. Dad was a chimney sweep who gave allotment holders soot to help their vegetables to grow. He was rewarded with gifts of vegetables left on the cottage doorstep. Then, when schools were closed for holidays, Mr Bottomley benefited from the extra work of sweeping the boilers.

Sparsely furnished, their cottage had a black horsehair settee, shaped rather like a chaise longue, with a raised head rest at one end – though how anyone could ever rest on prickly horsehair remains a mystery. Kathleen's mother sat on a rocking chair at one side of the fire, her Dad in an armchair.

Well aware of the straitened circumstances in which most of their pupils lived and the worrying expense of clothing even for necessities, Kathleen and the other girls were taught in sewing lessons how to make a pair of knickers. For a payment of tuppence a week towards costs, the girls were given three patterns to choose from, small, medium and large.

Kathleen's ambition was to join the Girl Guides. Prospective guides were allowed to attend without uniform initially, to see if they enjoyed it. Kathleen adored it. She was dreadfully disappointed when her mother had to tell her, sadly, that she couldn't be a Girl Guide – they couldn't afford to buy a uniform.

As they reached adolescence, Miss Wilkinson, one of their schoolteachers, told her pupils, 'If any of you want to know where babies come from, come and see me.' Kathleen had no need to go. She already knew. Out of mothers' sides. Another girl disagreed. She was sure they popped out from beneath ladies jumpers and cardigans. She had seen babies there. 'Nobody is ever going to cut *my* side,' Kathleen vowed.

One Christmas, Mrs Jarmain, who used to call at the cottage when she needed her chimneys sweeping, left a big brown doll's pram for Kathleen. At first she had only a decrepit old teddy bear to put in it, but her delight knew no bounds when, on Christmas morning, she found a doll that walked and talked by her bedside. She had heard about those wonderful dolls, but actually to own one! When school recommenced Kathleen would run home at dinnertime and proudly push the pram with one of the Wonders of the World in it halfway down Fenay Lane, to get the doll to sleep before going back to school.

Kathleen felt as though she were living in Paradise, and set aside special wash days for Dolly's clothes.

But Paradise didn't last long. Her Dad died aged forty-nine, her mother two years later. Fortunately the family lived near Aldmondbury cemetery, so the deceased could be transported on a wooden bearer, a kind of glorified hand barrow which considerably cut down on funeral costs. Friends lent Kathleen black mourning clothes. After the burial there was a 2 mile walk to her married sister's home where relatives had prepared 'a cup of tea and a few sandwiches'.

By that time Kathleen was working as a doffer at J.L. Brierley's mill down St Helen's Gate, Aldmondbury, earning 17 shillings a week. With both her parents gone she was faced with having to somehow or other bring up her younger brothers alone. She was up by six, attended to the boys, walked to work, then did all the domestic chores on her return at tea-time. There were so many clothes to be pressed that she had two flat irons, one heating on the fire while she ironed with the other.

At this stage Kathleen was fifteen. There was a shop in town, Whitfields, where people could pay so much a week towards buying clothes – a good idea but her meagre income wouldn't stretch to that. A hundredweight of coal cost 1s. 6d., she was almost at her wits end wondering how to pay for it. But kindly neighbours helped in many ways, telling the girl on Sundays, 'Don't worry about cooking a meal, lass. We'll send some across – no bother at all.' Without these kindnesses Kathleen doubts the orphaned family would have survived. Even so, she was desperate about coping financially. She walked into Huddersfield to plead for a shilling or two from the Corporation Housing Department – and was given the harsh advice to get back home and take her brothers to the workhouse at Crosland Moor. But that she would never do.

Others were almost as poverty stricken as Kathleen, but all were proud and dignified making the best of what little they had. Mrs Brook, who lived nearby, bought a cheap bit of stair carpet when her daughter started courting to smarten things up for when 'the young man' visited at weekends. It was put down on the stone stairs on Fridays, held down with stair rods, and taken up again when the weekend was over. Mr and Mrs Brook had one bedroom for eight but a cleaner family was never seen. It was a tight squeeze but they managed to maintain modesty – a large clothes horse with blanket flung over it separated the girls from the boys. At night time the wash kitchen downstairs was converted into a bedroom for the parents. Kathleen noted those conditions when Mrs Brook invited her in to 'have a look at Dorothy' who had pneumonia.

There were two brass fenders in Kathleen's cottage. The best was taken up on Sunday nights and placed beneath the other, so it would look spick and span for the weekend.

One evening she was expecting to meet a young man whom she'd been 'walking out with' for a while. Instead, a different one turned up – a 'blind date' for them both. The first young man, having been detained, asked his pal Arthur White if he would go and meet the young lady. Arthur was only too ready to oblige. The couple got on like the proverbial house on fire. Both had been orphaned and were making their own way in the world. As they strolled along the country lanes Arthur told Kathleen about his life.

George, his father, had had only one leg for years substituting wooden ones he made himself for the lost one. A bit of a character, George was in chapel one Sunday when Fred Langley came round the pews with the collection box. On special occasions George had been known to give as much as half a crown, but that morning he was 'feeling the pinch'. Nothing daunted, with a majestic sweep of his hand he mouthed 'No' to the superintendent. The young Arthur was mortified. Yet if the preacher didn't turn up it was his Dad, 'Oxford George' as he was nicknamed, who strode up into the pulpit and preached. So strong was his religion that he ate every meal with the Bible open on the table.

Arthur soon had Kathleen forgetting her cares. He recounted how he and his boyhood chum, Billy Raistrick, earned free ice-cream cornets – a real treat in those days. Fred Coletta found it hard work pushing his hand cart full of the delicious stuff up the steep hill from Deighton to Sunny View, so the lads offered to push it for him, and were rewarded with an overflowing ice cream cornet each.

Kathleen was entranced. Arthur sang in chapel concerts, once being encored five times after playing the part of 'Ah Sin', a

Chinaman. He gave a demonstration of the little Chinaman's shuffling dance to an enraptured Kathleen. He had no time to be bored. Monday evenings were for concert rehearsal when one was 'on the go', Tuesdays there were Christian Endeavour meetings, a prayer meeting Wednesday evenings, Thursday was choir rehearsal, Friday perhaps another concert or operetta practice. Most Saturday evenings there was a whist drive, social, or 'sixpenny hop' at the Sunday School. Besides all these activities, Arthur was a keen footballer. No showers after a game then, but buckets of water from the Sunday school sluiced down muddy legs.

Wolf cub Arthur White, aged about ten

Arthur used to live down Donkey Street, named after the donkey that was tethered there. He couldn't afford comics, but Walkers, who kept the off-licence shop, had three sons and a daughter (who had a club foot) and they let Arthur have their *Film Fun* and *Magnet* after they'd finished with them. He told her, too, how he had some Sunday school prizes at home, for good conduct and regular attendance. He promised to let Kathleen see

The football team outside Sheepridge Industrial Society. Arthur White is kneeling third from left in the front row

his copy of the annual *Chatterbox* and a book called *Sunday* next time they met.

The garrulous young man rattled on with great good humour about the well where horses drank and how he was 'laiking about' one day and fell in. At Easter his Dad usually managed to buy him a small chocolate egg, and they had a trip to the fair at Great Northern Street for a ride on the Shamrock, a sort of carousel, a coconut and bag of Fox's brandy snaps to take home. They thought nothing of walking there and back, a couple of miles or more each way.

He used to walk to Brighouse Swimming Baths on Sunday mornings, where it cost a penny to hire a pair of trunks and tuppence to go in. A treat when the swim was over was buying a 'Russian slice' from a shop near the baths. Then he would hurry back in time for Sunday school.

Kathleen wasn't bothered about not being able to get a word in edgeways – it was lovely to be entertained, and to have her mind taken off her problems. She knew there was always someone worse off – the poor soldiers, for instance, that Arthur saw marching up Deighton Road canvassing for other recruits going, as like as not, to meet an early death. Besides, it was such a comfort to know that she wasn't alone in being hard up – and making a joke, not a moan, about one's status in life was the best way of dealing with it. Like Arthur.

He had moved to Lepton when his father died, to live with his brother. From there he would walk 8 miles into Huddersfield to sign on the dole three times a week. Afterwards he walked back to Lepton again. He only had one pair of shoes and they had holes underneath. But he cut a piece of cardboard, shaping it to the hole, and carried identical pieces to renew on the hike. 'I couldn't feel the "causey" at first,' he grinned, 'with me new soles in.'

By the end of that first evening, the young couple felt as though they had always known one another. How she enjoyed the way he suddenly broke into song:

> On the road, on the road to anywhere –
> Never a heartache, and never a care,
> Got no home, got no friends,
> Grateful for anything the Good Lord sends

> On the road, on the road
> Every milestone seems to say,
> That through all the wear and tear
> On the road to anywhere,
> Will lead to somewhere, someday.

From then on Kathleen and Arthur both knew that life would never be as bad for them ever again.

But while Kathleen was out enjoying herself, her three young brothers weren't as happy. They daren't go to bed until their big sister came home. They were always waiting at the top of the yard when she arrived back from her walk with the 'young man'.

Love on the dole could be fun, given the ingenuity of a chap like Arthur. He hadn't a halfpenny in his pocket, but in 1932 he took Kathleen to admire a red sports car he'd seen in Newton's Garage.

'Would you care for a trial run, Sir?' the salesman asked the eager – and as he thought – potential customer.

'Er, yes, I think we'll have a look at it,' replied Arthur, ushering the timid Kathleen into the posh car. Off they went, a lovely run, all round Lindley Moor. Back at the garage Arthur scratched his head in undecided manner. 'I think I'd better go home and think about it,' he said with perfect composure.

When a hole appeared in one of his black socks, he'd no idea how to mend it so he put his hand up the chimney and put soot on his heel. Hey presto! No one could tell the difference. When his friends enquired who the young lady was that he was walking out with, Arthur's proud reply was 'a businessman's daughter'. It was quite true really, Kathleen's father had run his own chimney sweeping business. The couple enjoyed hunting for 'hairy nuts' in Mollicar Woods when they were hungry. Nuts that grew close to the ground, their presence indicated by small flowers.

Despite lack of material wealth, the couple had lots of laughter. Kathleen listened happily as Arthur sang his own version of popular songs of the moment, such as 'Sweet Peggy O' Neill'.

> Peggy O'Neill was a girl who could steal
> Any heart, any time, anywhere.

But I'll put you wise,
How you'll recognize
That wonderful girl of mine.
If she's smiling all the while
That's Peggy O'Neill,
If she talks with a slight little brogue—
Sweet personality, full of rascality,
That's Peggy O'Neill.

Then he substituted, 'He thought it was better, To have a French letter, For sweet Peggy O'Neill.' Often the words weren't exactly right, but that didn't matter at all. The melody was light-hearted, and easy to whistle.

Arthur and Kathleen married on 3 April 1933, a Monday, so that Arthur's brother, who was a butcher, could attend. Arthur had only £36 to cover the cost of the whole wedding. Ever economical, Kathleen was intending to buy a blue dress, from a shop next to Woolworth's, which she could wear afterwards. But Arthur was determined that she should have a proper wedding dress, and bought her a white one. He wore a black coat and pin-stripe trousers, which cost £3.

Girls from the mill where Kathleen worked were allowed out of work to see the happy couple emerge from church. 'Look after her, Arthur,' one called out. ''Cos she hasn't had anybody for a long time.'

There wasn't even enough money left for bus fares to work next morning so they walked from the rented rooms in Marsh. They had paid a shilling to someone for the address, which was a good one. Three bedrooms, a bathroom, 'front room' and kitchen for 12 shillings a week 'All in'. They hadn't to provide anything, not even towels or spoons.

Dole money around 1938 was 26 shillings for a married couple. Things improved and Arthur worked for a number of firms over the years. Eventually he was able to buy a motor bike and sidecar, and the couple zoomed off to Blackpool where Kathleen's uncle lived. He had a stall on the sands selling shellfish. They won a 'dolly' on Blackpool Pleasure Beach – but it wasn't a patch on Kathleen's Christmas walking and talking doll of her childhood!

Arthur White, 'Dolly' and Kathleen
at Blackpool Pleasure Beach

In the 1980s Kathleen and Arthur retired to Emley, near the
'wireless mast', where Arthur soon made a name for himself
roaming the Pennines with retired pitman Dennis Bowden and
another friend, George Gill. Twice weekly the trio teamed up to
act out *Last of the Summer Wine* stories. Who else for Compo but
Arthur who has always been short in stature. Dennis was Foggy
and George took the part of Clegg.

Those walks became the highlight of the week, only a few miles
from where the television series is made. After a 6 mile walk around
Emley Moor and Flockton – sometimes going as far as Cawthorne
– the happy trio used to pause for a pint at the Woodman in
Clayton West, finishing off with fish and chips. Arthur, as ever,
would do anything for a laugh. Wearing a woolly cap and
Wellingtons, he used to walk merrily to the top of a hill, then
charge down again like a two year old, flapping his arms like a bird.

Not having a Nora Batty of their own, George's English setter
Oliver used to enjoy the jaunts round the Pennine districts of

Last of the Summer Wine lookalikes. From left to right: George Gill as Cleggy, Arthur White as Compo and Dennis Bowden as Foggy

Clayton West, Skelmanthorpe and Emley. Before retiring Arthur was a chemicals supervisor at the ICI plant, Dennis an examining engineer, and George was a group surveyor. He was the one who organized, with maps and his knowledge of the districts, where they went for their exploits. A few years ago they were featured on television. A far cry from chapel operettas and 'Ah Sin'.

CHAPTER TWELVE

ANNIE OF CASTLEGATE

Castlegate and Northgate were rough areas of Huddersfield in the 1920s and '30s. In the main, this was due to the Irish immigrants who had settled there and who instigated fights on Saturday nights, when they enjoyed getting drunk. One public house was even nicknamed 'The Blood Bucket' (the Northgate Arms). Windows were regularly broken when bottles were thrown – from the inside. The only means of calming them down was the appearance of the Catholic priest.

In 1917 Annie Brennan was born in Kaye's Square, Quay Street. As a child, she adored scrubbing and washing the yard and knowing what an excellent worker Annie was, the rent man sometimes gave her a threepenny bit if she promised to sweep it. So keen on cleanliness was little Annie that she once borrowed her mother's bucket and went to scour Brierley's mill office steps, scooping water out of the canal. There were differences between donkey stones and pieces of ruddle, the former being a pale yellow, while ruddle was like a rock and dark yellow. Lodging houses used ruddle on their steps, but Annie's mother told her daughter, 'Get a donkey.' It made all the difference, the hue of one's doorstep, making one go up or down in the social hierarchy.

Greengrocer Aked Stewart had a proper donkey, and a cart from which he sold baskets of strawberries and gooseberries on hot summer days. When Castlegate children were on school holidays it was a nightmare for poor Aked. He'd pull up outside the Dog and Gun for a pint, and the youngsters then stole some of the fruit they would never get otherwise. Sometimes it was as though the donkey tried to warn him – it followed him into the pub, but the landlord chased it out.

Annie, Kathleen and Roland in Kaye's
Square, Quay Street, in the 1920s

When mothers went out for a drink on Saturday nights they never bothered to lock house doors. Annie and her friends preferred it when their mothers hadn't any money as then they were forced to stay at home. And there wasn't any arguing with neighbours, as there always was when they'd had a few drinks.

The children borrowed old, deep prams if none was in use at home, going in droves to the gas works, where they bought 'six penn'orth o' coke' to eke out the fuel. It was chucked straight into the prams. No bags. Sometimes they bought 'three penn'orth of coal' – a big bucket full.

One day Annie and her pals magnanimously offered to give a little girl a ride in one of those prams. Once she was inside, they set off, chasing wildly over the cobbles on their way to the canal. Quite forgetting its contents, they let go of the pram, which, as it gained momentum, tipped over, violently ejecting its passenger who cracked her forehead on the cobbles. Screams were heard all over Castlegate, punctured by horrified denials and accusations.

'It was your fault—.'

'No, it was yours—.'

Myra, the child's older sister, came rushing to the scene, and all of them hurried up to the Infirmary, fearing their mothers would 'slaughter them' when they found out what had happened.

'Tatters', people who went round selling second hand clothes, called with their wares on Friday evenings, pay day. Even at minimal prices, customers tried to barter them down. Annie recalls how she forgot herself one time and showed interest in a particular garment – the price was promptly escalated to a shilling.

Mrs Roddy had a draper's shop; she was never seen without a tape measure slung round her neck. It was from her shop, if they were lucky, that children had white dresses bought for Whitsuntide. Mrs Brennan bought Provident clothing cheques, one or two shillings worth when the collector came round, again on Friday nights, before wages were depleted at the pubs. Sometimes a useful garment came their way from Annie's auntie, Rosie Hever, who kept a second-hand shop on Castlegate.

It wasn't unknown for bugs to infest the houses in some yards. They seemed particularly attracted to horsehair sofas. If some of the furniture legs were contaminated they were stood in cans of creosote or paraffin. Before setting out for church on Sunday mornings people asked one another, 'Have I any bugs on me?' A worshipper might be in a pew, head bowed, and notice one creeping up a coat or stocking.

New babies appeared almost as frequently as did bugs. Nurse Mellor, who lived in Upperhead Row in the 1920s, was sent for when one was due. Or children were told, 'Go to the Irish League and get your father, and then Nurse Mellor.' At such times neighbours, though on the breadline themselves, were never found wanting; they were always ready to help when one of their clan was in need. They made a gruel, washed nappies, or baked a stone of flour when a new mother was 'lying in'.

Annie's home didn't possess a clock. If they needed to know the time, they simply went to look at the Co-op clock, or at the one on the parish church, or, even simpler, listened to the chimes. If they happened to be talking when the bells chimed they were in doubt for the next hour as to whether it was two or three o'clock. . . . Instead of an alarm clock there was a knocker-up on weekdays, Sally, who earned fourpence a week for getting workers out of bed in time for the mills' opening.

But their life had its compensations that, had they been rich, would have passed them by. Such as the time when the rag and bone man scuttled up to Greenhead Park wearing Mrs Brennan's knickers. It was one of those boiling hot days in the 1930s, and how he yearned for a pair of shorts instead of his heavy serge trousers. When Mrs Brennan suggested them as a substitute, both he and the knickers felt to be over the moon as gentle breezes wafted his bare legs. A very good shorts substitute – and an hilarious sight. Then there were allotments on Leeds Road where, if they took a bag, they could get a load of lettuces and radishes, for tuppence.

Most families couldn't afford fireworks on 5 November so they watched other people's bonfires. However, when Annie was eight or nine she was gazing wistfully into Snowdon's sweet shop, which had an extensive display of rockets, Catherine wheels, sparklers and Roman candles when a voice behind her asked, 'Would you like a box of fireworks, Love?' The mystery man paid two shillings for a box of assorted ones, his reward being the expression of sheer joy on the little girl's face. She clutched the box and ran home to Kaye's Square as though she had the whole world in her arms. Riches beyond compare, to share with her friends.

Annie and her sisters and brothers were entertained on Saturday evenings watching the fights between the Irishmen, out in the streets. On Sunday morning they were right as rain with each other, slapping old pals on the back whom they had been threatening to kill only a few hours before and asking with genuine concern, 'O.K.?' What's a black eye or two between pals – it's all in the course of a lifetime.

One day a neighbour asked Annie to look after her dog while she went to see someone in the Infirmary. How posh Annie felt, walking round with a dog on the end of their clothes line. So swanky did she feel that she walked all the way up to the hospital and back, so more people would see her. With a real dog. On a lead.

When not having the responsibility of a dog on a rope to look after, she played for hours on the War Memorial in the park. Or made a den down Milner's Yard, sitting on a bit of old carpet with a couple of candle holders and stumps of candles in the pretend house. Down the yard was a little wooden hut where children played cards.

A lot of time was spent going round houses asking, 'Have you any pop bottles, Mrs Clary?' or whoever came to the door. When the bottles were returned to the shopkeeper, they were given a halfpenny or a penny back. With a penny or two in their pockets the children felt as though they were millionaires.

Perhaps one of the biggest thrills Annie experienced was sitting up in the 'Gods' – less romantically, the gallery, at the Palace. Seats cost a tanner (sixpence), but it was cheaper if you went on Monday evenings.

Monday morning many went to the pawn shop, taking back their Sunday best clothes and whatever else might raise 'a bit of the ready'. One washday morning Mrs Brennan borrowed a neighbour's trousers and pawned them. Another time she took in the chopper, which was kept in the dresser drawer. Annie's dad would have 'gone mad' if he'd found out his wife had pawned the chopper.

Whiteley's, confectioners on 'Wappy Nick' in town made delicious cream and vanilla slices. If Annie was lucky and if she got there before anyone else had 'cadged them', she was given some of the ends.

At school, children in need were given breakfast tickets which entitled them to go to rooms on Northgate and be given bread and jam or 'bread and drip'. If anyone bought the *Yorkshire Evening News* or local *Examiner* they mustn't throw it away – Brennan's wanted it for a tablecloth.

Mr Brennan was a gas stoker at the gas works. What heaven when he was asked to work a double Sunday, then he came home with a big white five pound note. At such rare times of affluence one of the family might be able to have a new frock from Berry's in the Top Market – they stayed open till nine in the evening. They were even well off enough then actually to buy fruit on Shambles Lane, which made a welcome change from furtively snatching what had rolled off the stalls among customers' feet. Those with less ready cash could get fresh produce another way. Fruit and vegetable stalls remained open until nine on Saturday nights, and if there was a lot left over they almost gave it away. Sometimes they were able to enjoy a 'proper meal'. When they had a ham shank with mushy peas, it was Heaven on earth. First the delicious aroma welcoming the children home from school, then the sheer joy of tucking into it.

Annie recalls that 'babies never saw a "titty bottle"', it being cheaper to breast feed them as long as possible. When they were weaned they graduated to 'pobs', bread soaked in warm milk with sugar added. No such luxuries in Castlegate as special baby foods in tins. If families were having a big pan full of 'hash' like a Lancashire hotpot, the baby had a dollop too. Until they were toddlers, many babies slept in drawers on the floor. No drawers, then, for clothes, but Brennans' hadn't many clothes, so it didn't matter. After all, there were Roland, Annie, Kathleen, Mary, Billy, then Teddy to feed and clothe, while Mrs Stokes had eleven children.

When Annie's mother was asked if she would like a fur coat that a well-to-do lady had to give away, her reaction was not, 'Oh, how smart I'll look,' but 'Thank God – it will do to cover t' children's beds.'

It was a free and easy community. Everyone knew everyone else, and if ever a door was shut they thought 'summat was up – they were dead or something'. Poor they might be, thieves they weren't.

Annie started going to St Joseph's School when she was five. Being a Catholic institution, they were taught by nuns who wore black habits and big crucifixes dangling on to their chests. There were more than forty in the class. Children learned to write on slates, not in exercise books. If boys did anything wrong they had to bend over and were walloped with a ruler.

Those youngsters who needed shoes and whose parents couldn't afford to buy any because they were out of work, were given a letter from a school teacher. Annie often cried at having to wear those 'charity' shoes; three holes were punched in them to make sure people didn't get them to sell again. It was obvious where they had come from, the Cinderella Society. Annie tried to cover them up with the laces. There were queues on Byram Arcade on Saturday mornings in the thirties, so many children needing footwear. The process was humiliating – they had more or less to tell their life history, why their father wasn't working, and answer other, similarly intrusive questions.

Many had tickets for food as well. That was known as 'living off the Parish' or 'on the town'. Gallons, and Broughs, were the grocers in Huddersfield where poor people presented food tickets to exchange for basics such as tea, margarine and sugar. There was no sick pay.

All the gas stokers were heavy drinkers, so Annie remembers. Her Dad worked all Christmas Day in 1931, and his wife walked to meet him, pregnant as she was. It was as though she had had a kind of presentiment as he died only a few days later, on 8 January 1932. He was downstairs in his coffin, Annie's mother upstairs in bed with a new baby. On top of her grief for her husband, she was consumed with anxiety – widows pension was £2 10s. a week. There were black cabs at the funeral, and drinking pals from the Irish League Club walked, cap in hand, in front of the hearse.

The family never dreamt of going on holiday. Annie's world was Castlegate – the 'Best street in the world' she always called it. Honley, a village on the other side of town, seemed another country to her. But there were pleasures in life without having to trail all over the place. You'd only to stand outside Reest's 'meat and taty pie shop' gazing at huge, mammoth affairs with diameters the size of a table top, to be transported to Paradise. Especially if your mother had given you a dish and a copper or two to buy a portion.

Mr and Mrs Reest stood on guard, either side of their home-made creations. She had a 'right big bust' and he had on a long white apron. There they stood, doling out portions 'just like our mothers made – scrumptious!' Their place was near the London and Paris Emporium, where ladies could buy lovely flower bedecked hats for Whitsuntide.

A family named Cantwell, who lived down Dock Street, was known as the only family with sufficient means for the man of the house to be able to put his suit on on a Wednesday night to attend the Labour Party meetings. Every other chap's suit was in the pawn shop.

At Billington's, memorable for the large rugs hanging up outside for sale to those who could afford them, clients for their 'other' trade couldn't go in through the front door if they were pledging something; it was round the back for those not buying new. There were three men in charge, George, the owner, Stanley and Mathew. Annie recalled how Stanley used to say disdainfully, 'What do you want on these?' looking down his

Annie Brennan (seated) with, from left to right, Kathleen, Pat, Mary and Billy with Roland standing behind

nose at the pathetic near rag and usually coming to the withering conclusion, 'Oh no, you've worn them all weekend, I'll have to lower you.' Castlegaters lived in terror of having their goods and chattels 'lowered'. If Roland Brennan stood against a wall on a Sunday his mother yelled, 'Come away from that wall! You'll get lowered tomorrer!' If someone asked for 'two bob' they might get 1s. 6d. If goods weren't reclaimed within a year they were 'lost' and could be sold.

Some were too proud to be seen actually taking anything 'to the pop shop'. Mrs Drake lived down the pawn shop yard. She was conveniently placed so that if people left goods with her they didn't need to demean themselves by entering the shop and getting a ticket. Mrs Drake did it for them. She never shut her curtains – indicating 'Business at all times'. Other types taking things to pawn loitered in front of the shop window until the coast was clear, then they nipped in and out without being seen.

Claude Hill's was a well-known pawn shop. Providing a service like Mrs Drake's, Mrs Eastwood was what Castlegaters called 'a runner'. She wore white pumps, and took bits and pieces in for Claude Hill clients. For that service she might be rewarded with a copper or two, or a grateful 'Sithee, lass, get thisen a pint o' beer.'

Some items, however, were never seen in pawn shops. There was a busy trade in gas mantles before electricity was introduced to the locality. If Annie and her pals were fooling around in the house Mrs Brennan screamed, 'Mind that ruddy gas mantle' or it could have been sent flying.

Maggie Broadbent went in and out of the Brennans treating their house like a second home. 'Can I bath your Annie?' she might ask, grasping any excuse to be 'neighbourly' and get inside for a good old gossip. Helping each other in that manner didn't cost anything except time, and that was a commodity the neighbours were always ready to give. Talking and having a sympathetic ear to listen when life was at its worst helped many through bad patches better than anything else ever could. Laughing, joking, seeing the funny side of life were their riches beyond compare. Then Maggie Broadbent 'got off' with one of the young fellers who lived in one of the lodging houses, married, and soon had a family of her own to bath and look after.

Maggie's brother once appeared in the yard with a brick-red face on a bitterly cold morning, when its more natural shade should have been pale. 'Whew – isn't it hot?' he puffed dramatically. They'd run out of coal, or couldn't afford to buy any. So his father had come up with an ingenious if prickly solution. He had rubbed his son's face and hands vigorously with a piece of rough sacking or 'harding', as it was often called.

It was the Broadbents who had the scruffy little hut in their yard, like a hen hut. But for the children it was like Heaven, offering privacy and a place to escape from the grown-ups. It was where all the lads and lasses used to gather and gamble for halfpennies. There was no smoking or swearing among them, 'No bad thoughts either, just good fun' recalled Annie.

Houses were back-to-back which gave residents the advantage of never needing to feel alone and abandoned. If someone needed help, all they had to do was knock on the adjoining wall, and a neighbour came scurrying round. No waiting. Better than a private hospital really! Of course, there was another side to it. When heated disputes, even fighting and swearing and things being knocked flying were going on full blast in the next house, every word could be heard. Depending on how one looked at it, such excitement was sometimes more entertaining than going to the pictures – and cost less, too.

All manner of ingenious ideas were conjured up to 'make do and mend'. Saving money being as important, they knew, as earning it. No use letting hot water from the boiler run away down the plug hole willy-nilly – plugs were put in sinks as a matter of course. Hot water was too precious a commodity to waste. If there was no money for fuel, and no sticks available from the fields, dried potato peelings were not to be sniffed at as tinder with some papers to try and induce a bit of a blaze. Or, in times of desperation, an old chair leg would be chucked on the fire.

Children were only too keen to run errands. Annie remembers how she earned a silver threepenny bit from Mr Pickles, the cobbler on Leeds Road, a number of times. On Saturday nights grocers shops were a 'Happy Hunting Ground', youngsters running in to ask, 'Please, Mister, have yer any wooden boxes to spare?' Usually they had, and were only too glad to get rid of them. Here, surely, was something to thank God for in the Catholic church next morning – the knowledge that there was a stack of wooden boxes at home to keep them warm gave meaning to the hymn 'Praise God from whom All Blessings Flow'.

Life is, after all, largely what you make it, and you never know what good fortune may be around the corner. For instance, the Brennan family didn't have a full-length mirror, but if any of the girls were going to a dance or somewhere special, their mother suggested, 'Go and have a look at yourself in the Maypole mirror.' By this she meant the grocer's, down King Street, which had a kind of entrance foyer with a long glass at the side. Marvellous! Just the job if a lady was going out for a drink at the Elephant and Castle, or other pub, and wanted to know she looked her best from top to tail.

Most families, however near destitution, possessed a wireless. It was considered a priority, their means of keeping in contact with the world at large, and more convenient than a paper. Of course, trust it to break down just when the Wembley Cup Final was due to be broadcast. 'Go round and tell Harry Bushby' was the urgent call that went out if something 'needed looking at'. Harry repaired the Brennans' wireless, and it was propped up with a flat

Hope Bank, Honley

iron. 'If they put a bulb in they thought they were engineers,' laughed Annie. She remembers hearing King George V speaking to the nation on Christmas Day on that wireless, and thought it was wonderful that his voice should be in Kaye's Square.

In July, before schools broke up for the summer holidays, the headmaster of St Joseph's had an important announcement. 'Now then, hands up, who would like to go to Honley Home?' Although Honley was like a foreign country to Annie, her hand shot up nevertheless. She enjoyed going there, even staying for three months one year, but loads ran away. Mothers had to pay 2 shillings towards costs, but it meant a wholesome change for the children. Her own mother visited every fortnight, on a Saturday afternoon. Dads were either too busy working, or drinking.

At Honley Home girls slept in pink dormitories, boys in blue. They went for long walks in the countryside on lovely summer days. One teacher took them to Thurstonland 'to see the birds and the bees'.

Nurse Emily, who was in charge of the dormitory where Annie slept, had the task of keeping heads free from nits. Families were encouraged to buy saffron paste from Dodd's chemist to kill them off, 'Three penn'orth of saffron in an old pot no longer in use usually did the job.'

Annie and the rest of the Cinderella girls wore striped blue and white dresses. There were Liberty bodices to go underneath when the weather was cool, and black speckled pumps. Miss Winfield was the teacher, in charge of thirty girls. After walks outdoor shoes were changed for those pumps.

A Mr and Mrs Oates grew all the vegetables, and there were gooseberry bushes galore. Breakfast at Honley consisted of 'proper drip' in a big white enamel basin edged with a blue rim. It was spread on home-baked brown bread. Annie had never heard of brown bread until she went to Honley. (When she went home, a neighbour in Castlegate admitted to eating brown bread on a Saturday, as a treat.) And what luxury to eat with a knife and fork! At home they only had a few spoons and odds and ends. When Roland took a girl friend home for the first time she was given the carving knife to cut the meat on her plate, they'd 'run out of small knives'.

It seemed to Annie that they were never really hungry at home. There was always a big black pan on the open fire with something in it even if only bones. Rather like gruel, it probably took away the hunger pangs but can't have been very filling. 'And we all had beautiful complexions,' said Annie.

However, children were selected to go to Honley who would benefit from 'proper food' – and Annie was one of them. There, they sat at long tables to eat meals, with long loaves of home-made bread set out on a huge dresser – the bread didn't stay there long! At Honley there were roller towels in the cloakrooms and proper washing facilities; in Castlegate, they only had baths once a week, on Saturday night. How amazing to have more than one a week.

It must have been like living on another planet. Where marmalade was 'a fixture' on tables as was the Lyle's Golden Syrup tin, its distinctive green embellished with a drawing of a lion to denote its strength-giving properties. Annie had her reservations about that – she didn't want to turn into a lion. There was porridge for breakfast as well.

The Brennan children all had toothbrushes, but not always toothpaste. They used salt in its absence, or put a finger up the chimney. However unlikely it seems, soot was supposed to clean teeth.

The Cinderella Society played a big part in the lives of many children in the twenties and thirties. A few days before Christmas they provided a big party for poor children at the YMCA. Not all children in a family could attend every year, it would have needed the Town Ground had they all accepted. But those not allocated places accepted the fact that it wasn't their turn, and looked forward to hearing all about it from their brothers and sisters when it was over.

A certain number from every school were eligible and one Christmas in the late twenties Annie and Roland were invited. In a feverish state of high excitement Annie and Roland walked there from Kaye's Yard to enjoy a slap-up tea with lots of other children, all eagerly seated at long tables. But, for Annie the wonder was not the food or the atmosphere; when she first entered the big room her attention had immediately been caught by a dolly on top of the huge Christmas tree.

After tea was wolfed down the children queued to be given a present from that magical fir tree, weighted down with toys. 'Sweat was rolling off me' says Annie, remembering her anxiety as though it were yesterday. 'How I hoped nobody else would get that dolly.' Then she was at the front of the queue and Father Christmas asked, 'And what do you want?'

'Oh, that little dolly, please,' gasped the awestruck child. It was only a little celluloid doll, with a celluloid quiff over its forehead, but Annie clutched it to her, and no child in the whole world that Christmas could have been happier.

When she was older, she used to take three little girls out who lived at the Kaye's Arms in Huddersfield. She even stayed the night sometimes. It was only a pub 'but like the Hilton Hotel after what we were used to.' But Annie always considered Castlegate to be the best place in the world. Where neighbours rallied round one another, where, if the brush head dropped off and you hadn't sixpence to buy another one from Woolworth's, or couldn't wait until Saturday to get one, Mrs Cleary or somebody else would lend theirs and be delighted to help. As long as you had a piece of velvet and a tin of Zebo polish, a house made spick and span with that and plenty of 'elbow grease' – and plenty of love – it was as good as any palace.

Of course, you had to be kept up to the mark. The priest

might twist your ear if you hadn't been to church. But if you couldn't keep warm at home there was always the library to go to and on cold winter nights a chap with a cart went round selling hot potatoes about eight o'clock. People flocked out to the cart more 'for a warm' than anything.

Nor was pride lacking. One mother used to bang a couple of plates together at dinnertime to make 'next door' think they were having something to eat. When spring cleaning came round sand was strewn on the stone floors, all the furniture taken into the yard and the whole house turned out. Soda in hot water cleaned everything in sight, apart, that is, from the fireplace with its blackleaded Yorkshire range which was the apple of Mrs Brennan's eye.

There were occasional amazing strokes of fortune like the time Mr Weldrake, a coalman from Bradley Street, didn't know that a 10 shilling note was stuck to one of his cart wheels. It was retrieved by the sharp-eyed Annie whose mother held it up to dry, exclaiming, 'Thank God, now you can go to the Palace tonight.'

Annie had a big comb 'like a ruddy coal rake' and graduated to using curling tongs to put a frizz in her hair as she grew older. She enjoyed 'grafting' so much she used to wash the outsides of doors as well as the insides. The doors in their yard hadn't any letterboxes, the postmen simply threw bills or letters in the doorway, as these were never locked.

When they came home after school Annie and her brothers and sisters could never be sure if there'd be any tea or not. There was always a tea on Whit Monday though, after the 'Walk' with the rest of the Catholic children, those from St Joseph's joining with the ones who attended St Patrick's.

When the sun shone and it was holiday time for other people, trippers on charabancs took pity on the 'poor little beggars' and threw pennies out for the children. 'What a laugh – and they'd only be going to flipping Belle Vue – they'd never heard of Spain.'

'Bobbies', policemen, patrolled Castlegate every two hours and were not averse to walloping anyone who was up to no good, administering a thumping crack with their truncheon. Annie admired Irvin Walker, a policeman who wore big white gauntlet gloves as he directed traffic. It was lovely to watch him at his work. Like a ballet, with the traffic swirling round him. What day dreams Annie had, especially of one day buying a long mirror like the Maypole Dairy had. And being able to gaze at her reflection, all of it, from top to toe, in one go.

Living in Castlegate was an education – if not the orthodox kind. One could see Gipsy Smith lounging about on Rosemary Lane, clay pipe clamped between yellowing teeth.

If children had been good all week they were allowed to go to a Saturday matinée at the Star cinema and were given the price of a ticket. In those days it cost a penny to go in. But if they'd been bad the punishment was a stern, 'Right, you're not going to t' Star.' Tom Mix, cowboy, or Roy Rodgers, or it might be that thriller, *The Clutching Hand*, was denied to them that week.

However, Annie, on the whole, was a good child. And when the landlord inspected their yard, after she had cleaned it, he was so impressed he announced to her mother that 'You could safely eat your dinner off those cobblestones.' Even in the dim light of the gas lamp they shone after Annie had been at work on them.

When her children started going to the swimming baths from school Mrs Brennan cut one towel in two so two children could have something to dry themselves on. Everyone borrowed from everybody else. 'Can our Annie borrow your so and so's costume?' would be asked when it was her turn for the baths. The Brennan children didn't have nightgowns or pyjamas, only old stuff that was no more use for day wear. Poverty and cramped conditions were evident in the bedroom where mattresses were of straw, covered with a sheet or blanket. Three children slept at one end of the bed, three at the opposite end. When straw started coming out the word went round, 'Better start looking for a new mattress.' These could usually be had for nothing as shops often had some to give away, that had been used for packing.

There was one 'outside lav' for two families with keys hanging on a bit of string from an empty cotton reel. A horse and cart came round to empty the 'closets'.

The brass fender put down on Saturdays was taken up on Sunday night. Yet there was an innate joy to life – people went around whistling and singing. 'Sally, Sally, pride of our alley'. It could have been made for Annie.

When she left school, Annie worked at Jessie Lumb's mill. Later, at her wedding reception, which was held at home, they tucked into potted meat sandwiches. Then she went with her new mother-in-law to the Plaza cinema to see Gracie Fields in *The Queen of Hearts* while her new husband and his father went to the pub, first 'tapping' the greengrocer for five bob to finance the jaunt. Mrs Brennan, short of bedrooms, announced to the newly weds, 'I'm putting you on the landing tonight.' Annie recalls how, before the nuptials on the landing were underway, they all had fish and chips for supper, eating with their fingers from the newspaper bags. They slept with fish and chip papers scattered all over the place.

Life was improving, materially. Brothers Roland and Eddie became 'marvellous footballers', Eddie even playing for Huddersfield Town. In later years Annie experienced the high life when she accompanied her husband on a trip. It was a million miles from the Castlegate of her youth. They ate in the Waldorf Hotel in London where the waiter bemused Annie by handing round lots and lots of different bits of food. She had never heard of hors d'oeuvres, so, to be polite, and feeling somewhat nervous, she accepted everything. 'Lettuce madam? Mussels? Sardines? Prawns?' She said 'Yes, please' to everything. She daren't say no to such a posh gentleman, all got up in black suit and bow tie. She ended up with her plate piled high, and her husband glaring across at her disbelievingly as the food continued to mount up.

When asked what 'Madam' would like to drink, Annie saw nothing wrong in asking for what she usually had – 'Guinness, please.' The waiter returned with a tray of shorts 'and a bloody big Guinness in the middle'. Finally, the repast reached its conclusion and coffee was served. 'Black or white, Madam?' Annie smiled, a trifle apprehensively. 'Both,' she replied.

CHAPTER THIRTEEN

PENNINE ECCENTRICITIES

It would appear that those known as oddities often have more wit and sense than so-called intellectuals. A man addicted to blowing nocturnal blasts on a bugle from the top of Rashcliffe Hill was removed to an asylum. On arrival, he asked if the clock on the wall was right. When assured that it was, he asked his keeper, 'What's it doing here, then?' In Victorian Huddersfield a couple named their four sons Live Well, Fare Well, Do Well, and Die Well. They couldn't be accused of choosing the commonplace.

Holmfirth on the Pennine Chain has become synonymous with 'characters'. Long before the area became *Last of the Summer Wine* country, individuals roamed around who would have been locked up had they been further afield.

Joe Fox Dawson was born at Underbank, Holmfirth, round about 1868. He courted Emma Hinchliffe, whose father owned Hinchliffe mill. When Mr Hinchliffe found out that his daughter hoped to marry the woollen twister, who worked at Washpit mills, Mr Hinchliffe vowed that 'if our Emma marries yon chap I'll cut her off.' But true love triumphed, and the wedding took place. Although Emma's home was relatively well-to-do, she could neither read nor write. Families didn't believe in educating girls 'who would only wed and produce children'. So Emma made her mark of a X when she had to sign anything. But that didn't deter her from enjoying the *Daily Herald*.

Emma derived a great deal of pleasure from making up her own stories about the people whose photographs she saw in the newspaper, inventing tales about 'adverts or owt'. If her mind wandered to the macabre, she could turn her attention to the obituaries of famous people which had thick black lines round the death notice at that time.

Joe Fox Dawson

The couple lived at Kippax Row, a few houses built in a square with a large garden. Less well appointed, to Emma's way of thinking, were the few houses further on that 'just went nowhere' on the cobbled road.

Every Friday evening Joe raced greyhounds across Dover Lane, Emma peering out of the window to watch which way he went. She hated the way he commanded, 'Don't feed those dogs, 'cos we're running them in Dover Lane toneet.' Emma, upset at hearing them howling hungrily down in the cellar one day, defied her husband and took some meat and potato pie for them. They were probably as fed up of being cooped inside a dark cellar as suffering the pangs of hunger.

Joe and Emma had a son, Herman. When old enough he followed in his father's footsteps and worked in textiles as a scourer at Birkhead's Scholes mill. Herman's wife Clara kept having heart attacks. One day when she was rolling on the floor in agony her small daughter Ada, then only six, ran to get Doctor Edward Trotter. The doctor lifted the child into his horse and trap and they cantered back to poor Clara. She was admitted to the local cottage hospital, and Ada was bundled off to her grandparents at Kippax Row.

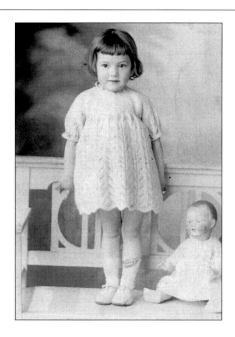

Ada Fox Dawson, aged about three

Mrs Lewis, Herman's cousin, lived nearby. A day or two later, walking back from school, Ada noticed that the blinds were drawn in her grandparents' house even though it was the middle of the day. Her father was there having 'meat and taty pie' – one of Grandma's favourite dinners.

'Your mother's dead,' said Ada's father, and carried on eating the pie.

'Go and see if Mrs Lewis will give you a halfpenny to spend,' Grandma suggested by way of consolation. Ada sat in a rocking chair after being given the devastating news, and rocked all afternoon. But she didn't cry.

When Clara was buried in Holmfirth cemetery there was one of the awful floods that Holmfirth was notorious for. Everything seemed to be cascading into the bottom of the street at the back of the Shoulder of Mutton public house.

After her mother's death Ada, who still lived with her father, used to dash home from school to light a fire and put the kettle on the gas ring for tea. Later it was considered better for her if she went to live with Grandma and Grandad Fox Dawson. Ada still has a letter written to her father by Tom Birkhead, in 1931.

Dear Fox, I was very sorry to hear of the death of Clara, and had no idea she was in such bad health. I enclose £3 which will help you to look after the little ones during this very distressing time.

Clara was only thirty-two when she died.

Another memento of early days in Holmfirth is a bill to Mrs Fox, dated 1887. It set out the costs as follows: for grave digging, 10 shillings; funeral bell, 1 shilling; hearse 7s. 6d.; one cab, 7s. 6d.; Total £1 6s. The sexton was E. Wadsworth.

Ada's brother stayed with Herman when their mother died, and their sister went to live with a relative in Barnsley. Ada attended Holmfirth National School. She took her father's dinners to the mill, in a pudding basin with a saucer turned upside down on top, a red hankie, like the one Grandad tied round his neck, tied over the lot. So before Ada could tuck into her mid-day meal she was always told to 'run across to t'mill

Herman and Clara (née Gledhill) Fox
Dawson

with this, love'. Dinners consisted of variations such as oxtail, vegetables, or stewing meat. While they couldn't run to best steak, there was often pig's trotter and vegetables. Grandma made brawn from cow heel or pigs' feet. Her Grandma also made Robin cakes. Ada recalls how, if they had a bit of sugar to spare, some was sprinkled on top of the plain cake.

Before the National Health Service was born, poor people especially had a stock of remedies to deal with common ailments. Herman had access to plenty of brown paper at the mill which he brought home if the children had bad coughs. A paste was then made from goose grease which was spread on the paper, a hole made in a sheet of paper for the ailing person's head to go through, and coats were then put on top. In winter, gaiters were buttoned up legs and clogs worn. They hadn't any gloves. Hands were shoved deep into pockets, or hot cinders carried in an empty mustard or cocoa tin to give a bit of warmth.

Ada enjoyed living with her Grandma and neither of them took much notice of Joe who could be 'an awkward customer'. If they were having currant teacake for tea, he declared, 'It's damned well good enough to eat without wasting butter on it.' Sometimes it was called 'School cake' because school children were given it after the Whitsuntide Walk. Their diet was supplemented in several ways but they only had salad if there was any in the garden, and they kept a few hens. In the kitchen the fire was kept blazing all the time to heat the water in the side boiler. When a piggin full of water was taken out, another had to be put back.

Ada's Grandma kept her mother's memory green by telling how she used to love going to Holmfirth market, and buy prawns wrapped in newspaper. She liked them so much she'd have eaten all of them before she reached home. Such cosy stories round the fireside, when Grandad was out racing the dogs, were what the little girl enjoyed best. Ada sitting on a square buffet, which was regularly scrubbed to a pristine whiteness. Their Saturday treat was a chocolate eclair each, from Pyrah's the confectioner.

To earn a bit extra, Emma did the washing for butcher Turner Mettrick. Ada enjoyed helping. If the spring water ran dry, they

Ada Fox Dawson, clutching her half-
a-crown won in the Bonny Baby
Show in Holmfirth

went to Well Hill, where there were two wells. If water was
running low they fetched it from there for drinking, in 'lading
cans'. There seemed to be washing going on all week, except, of
course, on the Sabbath.

On dark winter evenings a man toured Holmfirth with a horse
and cart, ringing a bell to alert householders that he had arrived
with McGowan's toffee bars for sale and other sweets. Emma
bought two tuppeny bars of Cadbury's chocolate in bright red
wrappers, sometimes putting them on one side till the Red
Letter Day of Saturday.

Joe hawked muffins in a wicker basket when in his sixties.
One day he would be selling muffins, the next tripe, disposing of
a quantity of his wares in the pub, its surroundings most
congenial to him.

A taste of fame and glory occasionally brightens even the
humblest home. There was a Bonny Baby Show in Holmfirth
when Ada Fox Dawson was a toddler, and her mother was alive.
Clara entered her pretty little daughter – and Ada won! Her
reward was half-a-crown. She had her portrait taken, clutching it.

CHAPTER FOURTEEN

HANNAH HINCHLIFFE AND BAMFORTH'S FAMOUS SONG CARDS

Some people's faces remain forever enshrined on old song cards, produced by Bamforths of Holmfirth in the early years of the twentieth century. One of these belonged to Annie Hinchliffe, whose father owned a gents' hairdressing business at Upper Bridge. Frank Bamforth went there for a penny shave and tuppenny hair cut when necessary. Here, too, 'private' customers had their own shaving mugs, bearing their names, arrayed on a prominent ledge. The Hinchliffe family lived at the back of the shop, their premises always bathed in a delicious aroma of lavender shaving soap. Mr Hinchliffe was busy until midnight on Saturdays because some wanted a shave in the evening to be prepared for Sunday morning chapel.

Mrs Hinchliffe baked daily, also making a rice pudding every day. When she had kneaded the bread dough she sent it round to the baker's, wrapped in a cloth in the clothes basket to be baked. She made all the clothes for her children, and brought them up strictly. They must never use bad language – or speak broad Yorkshire.

When Annie's mother married the choirmaster of Dam Head Chapel the choir had sung the well known song 'Sweet Lass of Richmond Hill' altering the words to 'Hinchliffe Mill'. The choir later accompanied the happy couple on their honeymoon trip, a wagonette outing over the Strines, near Sheffield.

Daughter Annie learned to knit socks at school, and never bought any from a shop in her life. When she was ten, Bamforths asked her to pose for some of their postcards. One was titled 'Jesus,

High in Glory', and continued 'Lend a listening ear, When we bow before Thee, Children's praises hear.' For another postcard, Annie and the other local children who were used as models were supposed to be begging. Frank Bamforth gave them bread to make it look as though they'd had it given by people who felt sorry for them. But by the time the sun came out to allow the photographer to begin, no bread was left. The models had eaten it all. Youngsters were given threepence every time they went to Bamforth's to be photographed for the song cards.

The Hinchliffe children adored outings. A picnic to Hope Bank Pleasure Grounds at Honley, taking Spanish juice in clean medicine bottles to wash down the sandwiches, was one such outing.

A great adventure occurred when Mr Hinchliffe hired a horse and trap to visit an aunt in Lockwood. When it was time to return home the horse refused to budge and Mrs Hinchliffe and the children were forced to go home on the train. As frantic attempts were being made to get the horse mobile, an old chap yelled out, 'Hoi, lad, tha's got its collar on t' wrong way raand.'

Annie enjoyed singing lessons, which cost a shilling an hour. Her teacher, Annie Brook, hired a room in a piano shop to tutor her pupils.

Annie Hinchliffe (left) posing for one of Bamforth's postcards

When thirteen, Annie Hinchliffe worked for Bamforth's full-time for a while, earning half-a-crown a week. This time it was ordinary work not modelling. But girls could earn 5 shillings a week 'reaching in' at Lower mill, so she later went there. Work commenced at 6.30 a.m. and finished at 5.00 p.m. with half an hour for mid-day dinner. Annie ran home for hers, and back again, in order to partake of the cooked meal; when she went to another mill her mother sent her portion of the hot dinner with one of the younger children. In those days a woman was employed by the mill just to 'mash' teas, a latter day tea lady.

Annie became anaemic, and a doctor recommended fresh air, so in 1915 she left the 'Dark Satanic mills' to become a children's nanny, earning £18 a year.

She remembers a touring company named Kelso's that had a member named Alf Foy. Like Annie, he posed for Bamforth's, this time for many of their comic postcards. Another comic was local blacksmith Fred Bullock, who used to work down a mill yard in Holmfirth. One afternoon he was filming with Alf and Fred 'Shiner' Beaumont (so named because he was a French polisher), Alf sporting a bear skin. They were sauntering back to Bamforth's studio when an old lady came out of a farmyard with a jug of milk. At sight of the 'bear' she dropped the jug and ran for her life. Another time a group of housewives were coerced into making a film. All they had to do, so they were told, was walk down the road. What they weren't told was that a hosepipe was to be turned on them! Those Pennine bred comedians could have been as famous as Charlie Chaplin had world events not intervened.

The Bamforth company was founded in 1870, producing lantern slides and romantic cards for a then eager market and only turning to comic ones after the First World War, when such sentiments seemed to have died with those heroic young men. Harry Bamforth went to New York in 1908 to carry on the business there; so successful were they that they even had branches in Chicago and Toronto.

Hannah Hinchliffe, born in 1887, worked as a weaver at Bottom's mill. She was a girl whose perfect features lent themselves admirably to the sentimental song cards. She appeared mainly on the

Annie Hinchliffe, ex-Bamforth model, aged ninety

sepia variety, often with local young man Ingham Hoyle, or the young Bamforth gentlemen. Christmas cards produced in those early years were more religious than the later kind and Hannah posed as Mary, with a Holmfirth baby as Jesus, on a card entitled 'Earth Today Rejoices'. The same card could be bought with the caption 'Emmanuel, God with us'.

In June 1907 a court case was filed in America after various publishers had copied and reproduced a line of Bamforth's 'Life Model' series. Hannah Hinchliffe, whose portrait had been copied unlawfully, was sent for and went out to America. The judge found in Bamforth's favour and an injunction was issued against the Anglo-American Postcard Company prohibiting them from publishing or selling cards known as 'Imitation Bamforths'.

At that time Hannah, known as 'The Most Beautiful Girl in the World', had probably been photographed more than any other girl in the world. Bamforth's had a branch of their firm in New York on Broadway, with cards of Miss Hinchliffe in a hundred or more poses. As some of the postcards were not marked for copyright, Bamforth's had no redress, but it was found that a chapter of the laws of 1908 provided that any person or corporation using the picture of any person for advertising or commercial purposes without written authorization is guilty of a misdemeanour. In 1914 the outbreak of the First World War stopped everything, including a hundred films destined for Russia. By that time Bamforth's were as far advanced as anyone in film technique.

Hannah and the other Bamforth 'Stars' are on permanent view in Holmfirth Postcard Museum. The beautiful weaver-cum-model married Fred Taylor, and lived in South Lane, in the centre of Holmfirth. Her sisters Martha, Lily and Edith also posed at the studio on occasion.

Marian Leake adored being brought out of Holmfirth National School to go up to Bamforths, frequently posing with her father, who was roped in on his way home from Newgate Quarry. Certainly Bamforth's didn't want him to go home first and get dressed up. The whole idea was to depict real-life Pennine people exactly as they were. It was perfect for Marian, who loved acting, even jumping in and out of coffins when a death bed scene was required. It was all part of the fun.

CHAPTER FIFTEEN

HARD GRAFT AT THE QUARRY

One of Marian Leake's friends was Harry Lee, who left school in 1906, aged thirteen. He started work at Gee's Quarry, Hillhouse Edge, his working day beginning at 7.00 a.m., with a ten minute 'drinking tahme' at nine, then dinner break at one o'clock till half past. Followed by hard graft again till five.

Initially, Harry earned 1½d. an hour and was paid on Saturdays. Good Friday was 'Rising Day' when the boss raised the 'nippers' pay by ½d. an hour for the young lads, with the strict warning 'We wants more work now tha knows.' No one was ever late; it was a matter of honour. 'Time's time, both for t'man and his maister,' reasoned Harry.

Such work always held the risk of accidents, hewing away at the stone as they did, unprotected. He contracted blood poisoning in his hands three times. But there was no pay if a chap couldn't go to work because of illness, even though it may have been caused through poor working conditions. Neither were they paid when laid off through being 'frozzen up'. Workers were open to the elements except for a bit of a cabin, and a stove which was acquired later. No smoking was a rule of the quarry, so the workers couldn't even have the brief pleasure of a 'fag' at break. On particularly raw days, Harry used to 'bat his arms' round his chest in a vain attempt to thaw himself out. Later on he joined Cartworth Moor Sick Club, and when the dole came into force he used to walk down into Holmfirth to sign on.

In 1920 Harry married, and the couple rented a house at Cartworth Moor, for 'two bob a week'. All the cooking was done directly on the fire. His wife 'bought a lump o' meat on t' Saturday, an' it lasted till about Thursday'. Then it was 'what tha could catch a' Friday'. Common fare was sheep's heads, which cost tuppence. When a child, Harry's dinners had been flour porridge with treacle, or if his mother was 'a bit flush' oatmeal instead of flour. And the usual drink to wash everything down with was water, and sometimes tea. After dinner, additional warmth in bed on bitterly cold nights was provided by 'oven plate blankets' popped into bed before retiring.

It was a spartan life, but they were 'happy as larks'. Harry enjoyed working – 'Just work, that's what life was all about, wasn't it?' Being content with doing a good day's work for a fair day's wage, not frizzling away all one's energies in stressful striking for more pay. Men took pride in their work, and asked for nothing more.

Every year for Honley Feast, Harry bought a second-hand coat, and a new pair of cord breeches, from Herbert Battye's. He paid 8 shillings for the breeches, and if they wore out before it was time to get another pair, 'ah just carried on with the old worn ones and got starved to de-ath.'

They couldn't afford holidays, so didn't bother thinking about them. 'Why traipse all over t'place when no one could have a better time than at Honley, Holmfirth, and Hinchliffe Mill Feasts?'

In summertime, there was plenty of pure fresh air and wide open spaces to be enjoyed. There was also cricket, a big stone serving as a wicket – and plenty more in the quarry where that came from. Pig and stick was another well-loved old game. Harry enjoyed the arts, too, singing, and listening to poetry. He remembered hearing the little Marian Leake singing 'Daddy' when she was a child, modelling for song cards at Bamforth's and singing in the Civic Hall. He remembered, too, the time a burial was due in Holmfirth churchyard, but conditions were so slippery that it was impossible for a horse and cart to attempt the tortuously steep hill to collect the waiting corpse. Indeed, some of those hills are almost perpendicular. But Pennine people are rarely defeated and the problem was duly solved by one bright spark who brought out a sledge, which was hauled up the hillside and then returned at top notch speed bearing its macabre load.

There were moments of supreme elation in Harry Lee's life, such as the time when a crane driver was required at Woodhouse

Marian Barrowclough (née Leake), a
pre-First World War model, with
old Holmfirth chum Harry Lee

Lane Quarry. 'Ah'll gie thi fourpence an hour,' the boss offered,
to coax the genial, burly Harry to change jobs and work for
him. 'That worra right lift, and ah stayed there for twenty-eight
years!'

A different kind of lift he never wanted might have come from
Fenella, the renowned Holmfirth tiger. The beast used to stand
at the back of the woman next door when she was washing up if
she forgot and left the door open. Frequently, when Wallace's the
grocer's sent deliveries, if the door was slightly open the tiger
came to investigate who was there. Harry was relieved when
Fenella died. While she lived, there was always the possibility she
might be at large. He was never keen about going up the hill
home in the blackout of the Second World War, especially as the
tiger lived on the opposite side of the road, and was noted for its
sociability.

Exotic tigers apart, there were more terrors in everyday life in
Harry's youth. One morning he and his pal Frank went out to
the two-seater 'Nessy' or closet as some termed it. They thought
to kill two birds with one stone, so to speak, as they wanted to
catch up with each others news. Once ensconced, Frank
wondered, 'How far can we get down Harry?' Both wanted to

be victorious, being at the age to accept any dare that was offered. Never a thought for possible consequences, Harry strove with might and main to push his lower body as far down as he could – so far, in fact, that he was unable to prise himself back up! He became stuck fast and had to wait until Frank ran to fetch his father. Fortunately, Dad was a joiner.

'Nay, lad, what's ta doin'?' was his opening remark at sight of the real-life comic postcard scene before him.

'What's ta think?' was young Harry's scathing reply. 'But it were nowt – there was no embarrassment about such stuff in those days.'

Shocks galore punctuated his life. One night Harry and his wife were in bed when they heard a continuous rattling downstairs. Could it be Marlowe's Ghost, come to haunt them in their hillside eyrie? Both knew that sleep would be impossible until the cause of the 'haunting' was ascertained. Being head of the house, Harry was commanded to get off downstairs and investigate. What a relief to discover that it was only the kettle lid that hadn't been replaced firmly! There it was, rattling on the hob as the water in the kettle simmered on the dying embers.

Ghostly tales abound in country districts. Harry recalled how, when a young lad, at Honley Feast time, once 'it thundered and leetened so me pals and me popped into t'chapel and went down t'steps underneath to lig there until it bated. A few minutes later there worra rattling sound, and we saw summat lurching down t'steps.' Their terrified gaze fell upon something with a white face, and draped in what seemed a white diaphanous robe. The lads shot out and across the graves as though the Devil himself was after them. But the apparition was only Mid-day Midneet, dropping in for shelter from the storm, wearing his white smock and carrying rattling milk churns. He was nicknamed Mid-day Midneet because he was lazy, bringing the morning milk round at midnight sometimes.

Another well-known character in the neighbourhood was a landlord who went by the name of 'Blow George'. His wife had gone to the 'Nessy' or privy and taken a square of newspaper from the nail on the wall. Unknown to the lady it was smothered in pepper and vinegar. It had, in earlier life, been draped round a portion of fish and chips. Shouts of dismay brought her husband scurrying to her side. 'Me arse is on fire! Blow it George, blow it!'

Understatement is peculiar to people born and bred on the Pennines. A labourer, shifting muck suddenly slipped, falling into the pit of a quarry. Catching sight of him, the foreman asked unperturbed, 'What the Hell atta coming down that way for, Ralph?'

Another lavatory episode occurred when Amos Kaye strolled into the outside lav then hurtled out again, white in the gills. 'There's summat queer in t' lav!' he yelled. When Harry went to investigate, it turned out to be the backbone of a sulphurous fish on the floor behind the door. The cat must have dragged it in.

Harry Lee's stepson Laurence was playing on the doorstep one summer afternoon in the twenties, when Frank Bamforth happened to pass by. He was captivated by the childish innocence and beauty of the boy's face and asked his mother if she would take him to the studio to be photographed. As a result, Laurence Brook's face was seen on calendars which were sold all over the world, with titles such as *Children's Hour* where he was portrayed wearing headphones to listen in to that popular wireless programme of the era. Laurence was rewarded with a

Laurence Brook, Bamforth child model, listening to *Children's Hour*

toy train and other playthings as recompense for modelling. How fortunate that he happened to be playing outside Hayfield Bank, up Cemetery Road, on that sunny 1920s afternoon.

As people began going to the seaside for holidays when mills closed down for Wakes Week, Bamforth's produced comic postcards for them to send home, employing artists to draw humorous situations, which meant they no longer asked local people to model for them. Arnold Taylor, born in 1910 at 32 Penistone Road, New Mill, was one of their artists and worked first with Douglas Tempest. Besides comic postcards, created in the Bamforth studio to the sound of his beloved classical music, Arnold introduced a series called 'Taylor Tots' in the 1950s. When not working at his drawing board, he enjoyed building dry stone walls, a traditional Pennine craft.

When commencing a new painting, Arnold first thought up the caption. But he never really enjoyed producing comic postcards, feeling he could have 'done something better'. However, his art encompassed much more than those, including birthday cards, with his name signed backwards, 'Rolyat'. He exhibited other types of paintings, and produced book covers.

An early contribution to the market in humorous cards were those depicting a fat lady accompanied by her much smaller husband. They were captioned as follows: *Little Man*: – 'I think I'm going to have pneumonia, lass'; *Lady*: 'Tha having nowt till ah've had a new hat.'

Arnold Taylor believed that Yorkshire is the best county in the country. There obviously was plenty of humour to be derived from the people who lived on the Pennines – at one time the artist was producing seventy-five new comic postcards a year, and wearing out dozens of brushes.

CHAPTER SIXTEEN

PENNINE SUCCESS STORIES

An artist depicting a different aspect of Pennine life is Ashley Jackson, who has a shop in the centre of Holmfirth. He prefers illustrating the bleak, often rain-sodden, misty moorland scenes. Though Ashley wasn't born in the County of Broad Acres, he identifies with it completely, even down to having the Yorkshire brand of humour. On the outside of the shop lavatory are the words, 'Kiss my Art'.

A 'war baby', Ashley is the son of the late Norman Valentine Jackson, who was General Manager of the Tiger Beer Company in Singapore. When Singapore fell to the Japanese, the ten-month-old Ashley was evacuated with his mother to India, and his father became a prisoner of war. He tried to escape, and was sent to a camp in Borneo. Finally he was handed a spade, and forced to dig his own grave. Maybe the melancholy of that recollection lives on in the bleak landscapes depicted by his son, whose work is now world famous.

Ashley's mother remarried, and they came to live in Yorkshire. Not renowned for his achievement in academic subjects, Ashley, then a pupil at Holyrood School in Barnsley, flourished under the influence of his art teacher, Miss Netherwood. He recalls how he won first prize in an art competition for road safety, then became head boy. 'Holyrood and Miss Netherwood made me the true Yorkshireman that I am,' says the artist proudly.

After attending Barnsley art school, at fifteen he became an apprentice sign writer. His bad spelling turned out to be a blessing in disguise; his many mistakes moved his thoughts into other directions where atmosphere, not spelling, told the story.

Ashley met Anne Hutchinson, married, and lived in a two-up, two-down terrace house at 27 New Street, Dodworth, a mining

Artist Ashley Jackson and his wife
Anne

village. Rent was 17 shillings a week. There was no bathroom and the outside toilet was shared.

Sheer grit and determination made him what he is today, a highly successful man, yet one who has never lost the ability to mix with both high and low brow. His rise to fame began in 1965 when he exhibited moorland paintings at a cheese and wine party in a private home in Brighouse. In 1967 he was elected a Fellow of the Royal Society of Arts.

Ashley opened his first gallery in Barnsley. What a thrill for him when L.S. Lowry called in – and bought one of his paintings! Ashley uses his talent in many ways. He has taught prisoners in Wakefield Jail, frequently appears on television, and Secker and Warburg have published his autobiography, *My Brush With Fortune*.

Ashley Jackson's paintings have been commissioned all over the world. But perhaps the main highlight of his colourful life came in 1987 when the Prince of Wales opened one of his exhibitions in Huddersfield. But Ashley never forgets his early struggles, and helps others whenever and wherever he can. One sketch he did for charity recently raised £120,000.

There are lots of talented people living in the Pennines – probably having more real talent than the hyped, media-promoted types in the metropolis. Not all can achieve fame and fortune, nevertheless those who give of their talents voluntarily contribute enormously to the sum total of human happiness.

Giving pleasure to others is what motivates the likes of Herman Sanderson, who was seventy-seven in October 1993. Herman delights congregations at Huddersfield's Leeds Road

Spiritualist Church with his unique arrangements of hymns when he plays the organ there every Sunday evening. What a surprise worshippers had when Herman launched into the tune of 'Hands, Knees, and Boomps-a-Daisy' to accompany the words of a well-known hymn! Herman selects all four hymns for the service, and is allowed to pick whatever tune he fancies for one of them. Provided that it fits the metre.

One of his favourites is Elgar's 'Pomp and Circumstance' march, lending the proceedings something of the atmosphere of the Last Night of the Proms. The organist jazzes it up or sways with undisguised delight when he has chosen 'After the Ball is over' or other well loved melodious tunes. He resembles the long-gone cinema organist in his maroon coloured jacket, reminiscent of an old-time band leader. Congregations ripple with amusement as familiar tunes have to be sung to more solemn words, swaying with pleasure as they sing.

The format inspires a far friendlier atmosphere than all the modern vogue for turning round and having to shake hands with strangers – or those you've already been talking to – prevalent in orthodox churches. So inspiring is his music that if Herman played at Lourdes, he would surely have the effect of making the sick get up and dance for sheer joy! Yet Herman Sanderson is far

Herman Sanderson in Leeds Road
Spiritualist church

from flippant. He prays every night, and also plays in old people's homes for no reward other than their delight.

After Dunkirk, he played for troop services at Adel Parish Church in Leeds. No one ever objects even if he thinks fit to jazz up Bach's 'Jesu, Joy of Man's Desiring'.

Showmanship runs in his family. His father, 'The Great Randolph Herman', was a singer whose main living was earned as a master baker. He died in 1916 when Herman was a baby. Strangely, when Herman first had piano lessons, aged ten, he hated them, putting the clock forward so it would look as though practice time was over. What he wanted was to be out playing with his friends.

Born in Berry Brow, he attended Golcar Church of England School. At fourteen he became a dental apprentice to a Mr Black in Chapel Hill, Huddersfield. For his job he was kitted out with a maroon page-boy style uniform, resplendent with chromium plated buttons. His duties were to answer the door to clients, and clean the instruments, to answer the wall telephone, and to put the names of patients up on the wall.

It was only when Reginald Dixon became famous, playing the organ at the Tower Ballroom, Blackpool, and the Sanderson

Herman Sanderson in the uniform of a dental 'page'

family bought a wireless, that Herman became enthusiastic about music. When he returned from serving in the Army Dental Corps during the Second World War, he played occasional evenings at the Brunswick pub in Lockwood. Then, music was not allowed in public houses on Sundays. When Herman did play, remuneration was 'ten bob a night'.

Another of Herman's passions was riding on the Big Dipper at Blackpool. Nowadays he only visits Blackpool on day trips – what would they do at church without their weekly treat of Herman and his original playing of the organ? He has stopped going on the Big Dipper, but still manages to stay 'On the Sunny Side of the Street'.

The weather plays a big part in moorland areas – get caught out in a storm and there's no shelter. Yet weather can be a friend as well as a foe. It all depends on how you harness it. The late Arnold Stead, born in 1913, harnessed the wind up at Helme, near Meltham, to provide a generator. He first started to build a windmill in 1958. There were various set-backs including the time when one of his attempts blew up in a 70 mile an hour gale in the early 1960s. He was convinced that he would not have had as good a final one had he not learned by his mistakes.

Arnold, then a chimney sweep by trade, maintained that hobbies keep a person healthy. Besides his Heath Robinson inventions, he played the banjo – 'a happy little instrument' – and also the string bass. He played in Herman Darewski's 'second band' at one time – 'He used to have us as t' mugs,' Arnold maintained.

Arnold Stead's philosophy of life was harsh by modern standards: 'Treat 'em soft and they'll never do anything for yer. Nor for themselves either. But give 'em a dose of hard times – let 'em be out of luck an' money, an' maybe health too – and that makes better men of 'em directly.' Initiative and the capacity for invention are often preferable to wealth, and make life more interesting, Arnold maintained. A perfect example of he who practised what he preached, Arnold took the wood for his Pennine Wind Machine from a skating rink that used to be in Meltham, before the days of silent pictures. 'You can nearly live, if you're sensible, on what other people throw away,' was another of his sayings. He acquired a door for his hut from a tip, as well as screws and handles – 'a tip stretching from here to Scarborough, so plenty to choose from!'

Character building, as well as windmill building, played a great part in the way Arnold regarded Life. 'People are kind o' like flowers, like yon iris when I throwed it onto t' scrap heap. It knowed it ud either have to git on or git out, and a bit of a shock like that never hurt anybody.'

Tenacity meant that he attended school for six years without missing a day. By 1934 he was playing music for money, keeping a record of his earnings in a notebook. That January, for three hours work, he received 7s. 6d., 7 shillings, and 5s. 6d. In 1936 he joined the Westbourne players, entertaining at various Pennine locations including Marsden Mechanics, Meltham Oddfellows, Scisset Baths, Skipton Town Hall and Brighouse Municipal Hall, the latter venue nicknamed the 'Sweat Box' by Arnold as it was unventilated.

In 1937 he worked in a mill doing a forty-seven hour week for £2 8s. At one period Arnold managed fifteen years without coal, using only wood he had cut from trees, or gathered, to heat water. During the Depression of the thirties he worked on a farm from 1927–37 in exchange for his keep. There was no question of wages.

It took him twelve years to build the Pennine Wind Engine to his satisfaction. He wanted one to power his own workshop machinery, 'If someone could fathom a way to save wind, and put it in bags, it would save the country millions' he used to say.

Towards the end of his life Arnold said of his forty-year-old banjo 'I laike on it now just to suit mesen.' He enjoyed playing tunes from the twenties, 'Leave Me Alone in my Dreams', 'When Johnny Comes Marching Home', anything with a lilt to set the feet tapping.

When a local parson suggested he might enjoy a visit to his church, the response was 'The woods are my church – where t'birds are singing and bluebells coming up.' Here is a final comment from the maker of the Pennine Wind Machine: 'This earth is like a seat in a cinema. We relinquish it when the show is over.'

Geoffrey Purves, chimney sweep,
with a black cat for luck

Few see the inside of as many people's houses as does a chimney
sweep. Contrary to what 'collar and tie' workers may think,
Geoffrey Purves would not have swapped his 'mucky job' with
anyone. He loved early rising – 'best time o't' day' – and the
cups of tea and gossip with which most of his clients regaled him
when the job was done and the dust sheets were ready to be put
away. 'You get till you're not surprised at owt, and take
everything in your stride.' He once knocked at a door, which
was opened by a 'big bloke' stark naked. Nothing on at all
between him and the early morning gusts of cold air. But
Geoffrey, true professional that he was, 'never batted an eyelid'.

While sweeping an old-fashioned Yorkshire range chimney
some years ago he felt a strange furry object in the aperture. To
his surprise, something shot down and streaked away.

'Oh, it's nobbut our Blackie. He goes there regular of an
evening when t'fires out,' laughed the cat's owner. There were
some side ledges which provided a snug hidey-hole at bedtime
which the animal found particularly enticing.

Geoffrey had plenty of opportunity to breathe in sweet
Pennine moorland air as well as the soot, frequently sweeping
chimneys as far out as Parkhead, Holmfirth. When a lad, he

remembers some householders putting penny squibs inside to shake the soot down. Others threw lighted papers up the chimney to set fire to the soot. And a few hillside farmers dropped hens down chimneys, their agitated flapping of wings in transit doing the job. When they appeared on the hearth, bewitched, bothered and bewildered, covered with soot and squawking like mad, they were unceremoniously chucked outside.

Geoffrey used to be able to get blowing wrappers from mills, but now so many have closed, the supply has ended. Some clients used to leave a key beneath a dustbin or some other convenient place if they weren't going to be in. But usually the arrangement was that the door would be left open. Not an unusual sight at one time, when honesty was more common than it is today. He did one such job, which later turned out to be the wrong one. So he finished up sweeping the chimneys of two houses for the price of one.

Another morning a woman, whom he assumed to be the lady of the house, complained about every preparation the sweep made. Geoffrey became so incensed by her arrogant attitude that he picked up his brushes, touched his cap, and declared, 'Madam, I don't wish to sweep your chimney,' and stalked away. Later in the day he had a telephone call requesting him to return. He had been dealing with the charwoman.

Perfectly happy in the wintry weather, Geoffrey enjoyed working in December, when children assumed he was cleaning their chimneys for Santa Claus, and they eagerly watched for the brush head to appear out of the top of the chimney. One little girl ran into the house, bitterly disappointed. 'Your head never poked out of our chimney, Mister,' she complained.

As with many tradespeople, work at home tends to be neglected and customers attended to first. One of his neighbours had occasion to dash round and tell Geoffrey's wife that their chimney was on fire – the sweep had been too busy to clean his own.

Mrs Purves never put soot-stained clothes in the washing machine. They were shoved into an old tub in the back garden, getting a good 'possing' in that every Saturday morning. Sundays were sacrosanct. A day of rest. 'Newspaper to read after breakfast, then spuds to peel for lunch.' A chimney sweep's life was such a happy one. 'Life's what you make it, isn't it?' has been Geoffrey Purves's attitude.

The majority of Pennine people don't go in for flowery language, preferring to call a spade a spade. Brook Whitwam was one of a family of nine. Aged thirteen, he earned half a crown a week working for a greengrocer. With a cart and Bob, the pony, Brook used to meet the tram at Outlane to collect goods sent from Huddersfield Wholesale Market. On Mondays he would fetch cockles and mussels, parading them round Bolster Moor, Rochdale Road, and Pole Moor. His call of 'Owt–?' could be heard a mile away, and required no further interpretation.

Later, when working as a twister-in for Hirst and Mallinson's, walking 3 miles to work and back every night for 30 shillings a week, he was sacked for chucking a bad bit of orange away. It accidentally hit the shed foreman in the face, and Brook was given his cards on the spot.

Brook loved to go on day trips, on a charabanc named *The Pennine Ranger*. One of his amusing recollections is of the Scapegoat Hill Band, which had a rehearsal room in a cottage, and was named Wheezy Anna as it always began with that song. 'Wheezy Anna, Wheezy Anna, down where the water melons grow. . . .'

Perhaps the environment and place one lives in does have an effect on people. Church Street, Golcar, had the alternative name of Bonkers Hill. We all know what 'going bonkers' means. Alf O'Bonks, real name Alfred Taylor, was an eccentric bachelor who never did a day's work after the age of twenty-three. He was supposed to have a bad heart, but he nevertheless creaked on – decked out in Edwardian-style clothes which he made himself – into his eighties. He was a keen member of Colne Valley Beagles and they still award an Alf Taylor Cup in his memory.

His cardigan was covered with so many patches, it was hard to tell what was the original material. He'd buy a chop and eat the lean bit one dinnertime saving the fat for the next day. He'd an acknowledged mean streak – he'd 'nip a currant in two', but then have sudden bursts of generosity, baking Christmas cakes and sending them to relatives in America. One wonders whether the recipients ate the gift from Bonkers Hill, or did the American birds?

Like many queer folk, Alf was a creature of habit. His peggy tub, posser and mangle were hauled up from his cellar every Sunday night in readiness for his Monday washing. On winter nights he wore his Ganzi (cardigan) in bed, sitting up and sipping a tot of whisky before going off to sleep. His father had once visited a Harley Street specialist in 1910, and Alf never forgot that it cost 25 guineas to be advised to sip a drop of whisky every night in bed. Alf kept on with the advice so as to get his money's worth from the tip! He did have some outdoor pursuits, too. Otter hunting was a hobby of Alf's, for which he wore full hunting regalia.

Zilpha, Alf's mother, was bedridden during her final years. She and her son played draughts every night, setting the board up on her bed. If he was doing the talking, he'd switch off his hearing aid to save the battery.

Village eccentrics were the target for buffoonery by local youths. One evening Derrick Whitwam, who lived at Scapegoat Hill, took a short cut through Alf's territory when he was on his way to meet his sweetheart, Annie. Alf happened to be on the roof of his house, spying out the land.

'Gerrof the other way round!' bellowed Alf, when he caught sight of the trespasser. Derrick's response was to remove the ladder. Leaving the old boy stranded.

CHAPTER SEVENTEEN

TALES OF THE UNEXPECTED

Across the Pennines, in Bolton, a television star emerged in the 1980s in the shape of Fred Dibnah, steeplejack. Having a sound aptitude for cabinet-making he was encouraged to find work with an undertaker when he left school. 'But ah took one bloody look at t'coffins and that were it. Ah was off as fast as ah could t'other way,' laughed Fred.

Fred's independence and individuality surfaced in other ways. Part of his National Service was spent at Catterick Camp. Once he walked the entire stretch from Scotch Corner to Bolton when he couldn't hitch a lift. But it was in the 'away from it all' world, high on the rooftops, overlooking Bolton that Fred found his true forte – as a jokey, nonchalant, completely fearless steeplejack. Monarch of all he surveyed.

Fame crept up on Fred as he was repairing the Town Hall clock. A television crew recorded his deft manoeuvres and cheerful commentary as he scaled the heights, as he precariously yet dexterously negotiated the seemingly never ending perpendicular ladders into the far blue yonder.

Fred's other obsession was with steam tractors, and he has been filmed driving those. His television appearances and ensuing popularity led to the flat-capped 'lad from Bolton' being invited to appear in beer commercials, advertising Whiteley's Brewery. Also to open fêtes. He was even one of the judges at a Glamorous Grandmother competition. The late Russell Harty was another of the judges, who was greatly amused when Fred remarked, 'I don't remember Grandmas looking like that.'

Though apparently immune to danger and injury when up in the clouds, Fred once fell off a pair of steps when decorating one of his daughter's bedrooms – and was knocked unconscious.

Fred Dibnah standing alongside his
steam traction engine

He said he enjoyed the life of a steeplejack mainly because 'up
there I can forget the bloody world. We live in a world of plastic
men and plastic drainpipes these days.' He thinks that chimneys
on the Yorkshire side of the Pennines have been looked after
better than those in Lancashire.

Though undeterred by heights, it is doubtful whether even Fred
Dibnah would relish the idea of befriending an orphan fox. But
that's exactly what a family in Thurstonland did. They allowed it
to sprawl on the settee in the front room while being fed with
fish and chips. It used to be taken for walks on a dog lead. An
old Ford Anglia was bought for the sole purpose of providing
comfortable quarters for their other pet, a Dobermann dog.
With the front seats removed, it made an excellent up-market
kennel. The car windows were regularly cleaned so that the dog
enjoyed good, clear views of the surrounding countryside.

Fish and chips being an integral part of the Pennine diet, it
was not really surprising when one man, used to having a 'fish

Sign on the local moors advertising
Home Fed Pork

and a penn'orth' with his wife every Saturday night in the 1920s, began eating them on her grave after she departed this life.

Even when Pennine people pass on, some seem loath to move on to pastures new. One tale in particular illustrates this phenomenon. On the bleak, isolated moorland road to Greenfield, near Harden Moss, stands The Huntsman inn. A sign on the roadside advertises joints of pigs available – 'We sell owt baa squeak.'

Folk tell how an overnight guest, returning late to The Huntsman, had to walk through the bar on the way to his bedroom. There he encountered a little lady, wearing old-fashioned wire spectacles and a long black dress, her hair scraped back into a bun. She was accompanied by a child of about ten, in knickerbocker suit, belted jacket, buckled shoes and hair in page-boy fashion.

The ghosts have been seen by others, but only rarely. The building is so old that the original doorways into the dining-room can be hazardous if one is tall and forgets to stoop. People seemed to be smaller in earlier days.

Up at Nont Sarah's, the pub within a stone's throw of Scammonden Dam, a ghost favours the cellar. 'Nont' is a colloquial form for aunt.

Tradition has it that in the middle of the nineteenth century a native of Scammonden took over the moorland hostelry, then named the Coach and Horses. Although it was in a dilapidated condition, the new landlord was too hard up to restore it. But since it would hardly entice business in so sad a state, the landlord was forced to try any expedient. Then he thought of his Aunt Sarah, who, being swiftly acquainted with her nephew's penury, was generous enough to assist him financially. Thereafter,

'Nont Sarah's', Scammonden, Huddersfield, a favourite place for an outing

in deep gratitude to his benefactress, the landlord talked incessantly about his dear 'Nont Sarah'. About 1870, a Mrs Sykes took over the tenancy, and had the name officially changed to Nont Sarah's, even allowing herself to be addressed as Nont Sarah by the inn's habitués.

A landlord of recent years, Brian Snooks, went into the cellar to change a barrel one snowy night. 'A mist suddenly drifted towards me, and the atmosphere went icy cold,' he shuddered. When he returned to the bar, one of the drinkers exclaimed, 'You look as if you've seen a ghost, Brian, lad.' The flabbergasted landlord panted, 'Well – I have.'

There's a poem that goes:

> Our birth is but a sleep and a forgetting:
> The Soul that rises with us, our life's Star,
> Hath had elsewhere its setting,
> And cometh from afar:

The souls who decide to inhabit Pennine territory usually arrive with an ability to speak plainly and bluntly, with no flattery or flowery phrases. Messages on old postcards sent by Pennine people years ago say it all.

In September 1904 Ellen wrote to Miss Lodge who was on holiday in Blackpool, furnishing her with the latest home news. 'Thanks for P.C. Glad your eyes are better. Polly got married on Monday and was very plain.'

People in the Pennines face problems head on – in June 1912 a Mr Kitson wrote on a postcard bearing a green halfpenny stamp addressed to Mr Wetherill, 31 Spencer Place, Roundhay Road, Leeds: 'Dear Sir, Owing to difficulties this week, I will forward you this month's rent next Friday night without fail, and 5/- off the old.'

Circumstances failed to improve, so Mr Kitson wrote again. 'Sir, I will send you my rent next Monday without fail. No work this week.'

Pennine people, like Mr Micawber, are ever optimistic that 'summat 'll turn up'. Before the prevalence of high-powered technology, when life ran at a more leisurely pace, all could partake in contests and games – however humble – and have as much chance as the next to win. For instance, the Woolpack held a competition one evening – a prize for the customer who presented the longest blade of grass. Another competition was for the best cabbage.

One of the locals, Randolph, worked at L.B. Holliday's. He took his cabbage there, and secretly dyed it a brilliant magenta. Though winning first prize for the exotic vegetable, his was something of a hollow victory. Knowing the history of that wonderful colour, he simply dare not eat it.

A cautious chap, he courted his young lady for forty-six years before they wed. Even the three-piece suite, bought in a sale and stored in his attic at the onset of the romance had disintegrated and gone mouldy before it could be used. When asked why he had waited so long Randolph replied 'Well, tha wants to be *sure*.'

In 1927 a Mrs Horton received a somewhat ambiguous communication: 'All being well, mother and I are coming to Huddersfield tomorrow after dinner. May call to see you, don't make a fuss. But don't stay in. With best love, E.J. Riddle.' What are the odds that Mrs Horton did 'make a fuss'? That's what Pennine people enjoy doing. There'd most likely be tinned salmon for tea, gooseberry 'cow' pie, rhubarb and custard, and a bit of Robin cake to finish off with.

ACKNOWLEDGEMENTS

My thanks to the following for assistance with *Pennine People*:

Miss Clarice Haigh, Mrs Lilian Haigh, Mr and Mrs Horace Hirst; the late Mr Arthur Howard, Mrs Jenny Ellison, the late Mrs Marjorie Motley; Mrs Ada Marston (née Truelove), Mr and Mrs J. Mellor, Mrs Celia Smith; Mr and Mrs Arthur White, Mrs Annie Myers, Mrs Ada Roscoe; the late Annie Hinchliffe and Marion Barrowclough; the late Mr Harry Lee; Mr Brian Snooks; Mr George Mitchell and 'Glen'; Mr Derek Walker, Mr Ashley Jackson, Mr Herman Sanderson and Mr Fred Dibnah; Mr Geoffrey Purves; the late Mr Arnold Stead; Mr Brook Whitwam, Mr and Mrs Derrick Whitwam; Mrs Mildred Burton; Mr Denis Wood; the *Huddersfield Examiner*.

Thanks also to the NCB Yorkshire Regional Coal House, Doncaster, and Bamforth's Postcard firm. My husband Granville, for assistance with domestic chores and chauffeuring me to often outlandish areas. Finally, to the Pennine locality itself for helping to breed such fascinating characters. (If any have been inadvertently omitted, doubtless they will let me know in no uncertain manner!)